Divinely Connected: Steps to Fearless Financial Freedom

Dr. Chonta T. A. Haynes

Copyright © 2020 by Dr. Chonta T. A. Haynes.

| ISBN: | 978-0-9991733-5-0 | EBook |
| ISBN: | 978-0-9991733-4-3 | Paperback |

All rights reserved. No portion of this eBook or Paperback may be reproduced, stored in a retrieval system, or transmitted in any form or by any means – electronic, mechanical, photocopy, recording, scanning, or other – except for brief quotations in critical reviews or articles, without the prior written permission of the copyright owner.

Unless otherwise noted, all Scripture quotations are taken from the Holman Christian Standard Bible ®, Copyright © 1999, 2000, 2002, 2003, 2009 by Holman Publishers. Used by permission. Holman Christian Standard Bible ®, Holman CSB ®, and HCSB ® are federally registered trademarks of Holman Bible Publishers.

This book was printed in the United States of America.

To order additional copies in any format, contact:

Heart 2 Heart Truth Ministries, LLC

1-813-299-2742 or 1-813-986-9660

www.ChontaHaynes.com

H2HTruth.org

Other Books by Dr. Chonta T. A. Haynes:

Not Just Paper

Financial Wisdom For Financial Freedom

Family Worship: Reaching All Who Attend

Special discounts are available on quantity purchases by corporations, associations, educators, and others. For details, contact the publisher at the above listed address.

U.S. trade bookstores and wholesalers: Please contact Heart 2 Heart Truth Ministries Tel:(813)299-2742 Fax:(813)986-9660 or email drhaynes@h2htruth.org

My encouraging inspirational sisters who are walking this last journey with me:

Machelle Haynes, Jacquelyn Bogen, Joyce Hare, Pamela Minor and Artricia James-Heard

Thank You!

How to Use:

Prayers: Take the challenge of 7 days asking God for divine intervention. Sign up at https://h2htruth.org/7-day-prayer-challenge for daily emails including memes and songs.

Come back as often as you like... He's waiting for you!

Devotional: Read, underline and get in tune with God. Focus on God and His character first. See Him working even when you didn't think He was working. Be open to watch Him turn your life completely around. The week's focus will be given as an indication of what area to concentrate on. Step by Step you will begin to walk in victory!

Planner: Jot down what you are working on this week. Include your business, job, family and relationships. Of course your finances will be highlighted. Use the notes section to write any thoughts from the devotion, any revelation God gives you, and as a gratitude journal. This is your space to dream... Dream Big!

This is your focus ⟶ *# 1 Goal for the Week*

TOP 3 TASKS

- ○ _____ ⎫
- ○ _____ ⎬ Concentrate on these main tasks to feel accomplished
- ○ _____ ⎭

OTHER TO-DOS: **NOTES:**

Mindset _____   ** Praise

Goals   _____   ** Gratitude

Budget _____   ** Ideas

Spending _____

Eliminate _____

Automate _____

Debt _____   Highlight any area

Credit _____   identified in the

Giving _____   thought for the

Savings _____   week

Investing _____

Business _____

Relationships _____

Family _____

Self Care _____

Internal work: To be most effective, sit with the devotion for at least 20 minutes, preferably in nature. Be still and allow God to speak to you and give you the answer. You will find that the specifics will come to you for that week. Expect to receive direction. Relationship is a two-way street; it's not just us asking, it requires that we listen.

Divinely Connected: Steps to Fearless Financial Freedom

7 Day Prayer Challenge:
For email delivery including memes and songs:
https://www.h2htruth.org/7-day-prayer-challenge

Day 1

Most Gracious and Heavenly Father,
You chose me before the foundation of the world, for that I am grateful. Your thoughts are not mine yet I want to think like you. You have a great plan for me and no enemy can mess it up. Help me to see myself and my financial situation through your eyes. Give me wisdom to walk in the abundant blessings you've planned. I stand ready to receive all that you have for me. My arms are wide open, ready to receive!

Calm my fears. You said to be anxious for nothing but pray about everything. So I ask for divine favor, blessing and wisdom so that I can walk into the abundant life you have planned. Renew my mind according to your Word. Show me, in the days to come, what I have been doing that has caused my predicament. Align me with the right individuals and systems to correct my thinking. I come asking you because you know all and are able to open doors that no man can shut. You are able to break down walls and part seas. Lord, I'm ready for you to intervene, so I thank you in advance.

It's in the mighty name of Jesus that I pray and give you thanks. Amen.
** Feel free to make this plural for the family (i.e. I change to we; me change to us; mine change to ours; my change to our)

Divinely Connected: Steps to Fearless Financial Freedom

Day 2

Lord,
You have all wisdom. Nothing catches you by surprise. You know the end before the beginning and everything in between. You are God and besides you there is no other. When it comes to wisdom, you've given us your divine guidance through your word. You said if we lack wisdom, all we have to do is ask and you will give it to us liberally. So today wise God, I come seeking wisdom regarding the systems of the world. I've found myself trapped in some cases and caught in others. Open my eyes to see the trappings of the enemy that hold me bound to unnecessary wasteful spending. Show me the right connections so that I'm not caught by alliances that aren't to my benefit. Break every chain that binds me. Free me from the bondages of thought processes that get me into debt. Release me now and give me divine council. I need to hear from you and I need your direction.

Lord, you promised to make me lie down in green pastures and lead me beside still waters. Restore my soul and my finances. What I have squandered let it return. What has been stolen, bring it back. What I have lost, help me recover. Where I have messed up, forgive me and set me on the right track. Jesus came to destroy the works of the enemy and that He did. Show me, teach me, lead me so that I will not fall prey to the world's systems at the enemy's direction. In some cases, the enemy came up against my finances but you promised that no weapon formed against me shall prosper. I will win and everything attached to me will win. Thank you for victory now. Thank you for opening doors for me and leading me into abundance. Thank you for the winning mindset and for renewing my mind according to your word. Thank you for intervening on my behalf.

I thank you for loving be back to more than enough because the price has already been paid by Jesus. It's in that mighty name that I pray and give you thanks. Amen.

Day 3

Omniscient Father,
Today I come knowing that you know my name. You formed me and have searched me. You know my down-sitting and my uprising. You know my thoughts. Because you know me better than I know myself, I ask that you show me myself. Reveal to me the areas I need to change. If it's my thoughts, correct them. If it's my speech, guard my tongue. If it's my behavior, arrest me so that I only do what you would have me do.

I come today asking for balance. Balance in every area of my life and especially as it relates to my finances. Help me not spend more than comes in and show me how I'm out of balance. Allow me to give passionately, spend appropriately, and save intentionally. Show me your ways as it relates to your Kingdom so that I am a asset and not a liability. Help me to know your name more fully and walk in victory because you hold my hand.

I believe you God and I believe your word. I thank you for access to your throne because of the power in the name of Jesus. It's for your glory I pray your hand release a financial breakthrough. I want to be free. Thank you in advance for financial freedom by the power of Jesus' name. Amen.

Day 4

Ever Wise and Wonderful God,
I come before you recognizing you said eye has not seen and ear has not heard neither has it entered into the heart of man what you have planned for me. You are a gracious and wonderful God. You sent Jesus so that I can live an abundant life. Your desire is for me to prosper and be in good health even as my soul prospers. You have been my shield and my source. Thank you God for all that you've done in the past and all that you continue to do in blessing me abundantly. I have life, health, strength, joy and favor because of you.

I come today asking for wise counsel as it relates to saving. You said a good man leaves an inheritance for his children's children. Help me make wise investments so that my legacy will be secure. Show me how to sow appropriately in the Kingdom and also to sow into my family. Teach me to put aside money to wisely distribute it and bless others. You made me to be blessed and to be a blessing. Make my barns plentiful not to hoard but to be a blessing. Thank you in advance for the more than enough life. It's because of the sacrificial Jesus that I claim my life and that more abundantly. Amen.

Divinely Connected: Steps to Fearless Financial Freedom

Day 5

Preeminent Father and Creator of All,

I come today realizing that you should have first place in my life and my finances. My first thought Lord is to thank you for what you have already provided. I'm truly grateful for the protection and provision you have afforded me. All the rainbows, new skies, tender mercies and material things you have allowed me to see, are reasons to give you praise. I make room for you in my life because you are my source. Without you I can do nothing but because of you I can do all things through you giving me strength. Move out of the way anything that takes your rightful place.

You know all things. You know that sometimes I've over spent. In some cases, I have gotten into contracts that now eat away at my ability to live abundantly. I want out of the land of just enough. Help me to pay my bills on time and to have the right mindset. You said the wicked borrow and don't repay. I don't want to be wicked. You said the righteous show mercy and give. My desire is to be righteous.

Lord, you told me to seek first your Kingdom and all things I need will be added. I come seeking your Kingdom today and asking for release from the bondage of spending and debt. I want to be in right standing with you. It's in the most gracious generous name of Jesus that I pray and give you thanks. Amen.

Day 6

Heavenly Father,
Goals and dreams fill my head tonight. I want to dream big and it begins with realizing nothing is impossible for you. Help me fully grasp your ability to change my situation as I follow and put into practice your Word. Give me dreams and visions tonight of my future that I can grasp. Wow me tonight and the days to come with divine visions of my future.

Purpose in my heart the desires you have for me to fulfill. Show me what to desire. You said write the vision and make it plain that others may run to do it. Reveal to me the vision for my life and my family. Give me clear understanding of my purpose and giftings and how they can be used for Kingdom purposes. In the name of Jesus and the power in that name I pray and praise your name. Amen

Day 7

Most Gracious Father,
Your desire is for a covenant relationship with me. You thought enough of me to die for me. I thank you for loving me that much. Your covenant promises allow me to feel secure and safe knowing you have my best interest at heart. I desire to keep covenant with you, all of the covenant. Teach me your commands and statues as it relates to finances. I will support the Kingdom so that I can bring glory to your name.

Father I desire to please you. Reveal your promises to me and help me stand firm on each one. I am your child and I trust you. I walk out now ready to proclaim to all the testimony that you did it for me. Give me a great testimony and opportunity to share with others what I've experienced, heard, read, and know of you.

It's in the matchless wonderful covenant keeping name of Jesus that I pray knowing you hear me. I am confident in you. Amen.

Divinely Connected: Steps to Fearless Financial Freedom

1 John 5:14 -15 "Now this is the confidence we have before Him: Whenever we ask anything according to His will, He hears us. And if we know that He hears whatever we ask, we know that we have what we have asked Him for."

It's time to believe what God said! The God we serve is mighty and able to do the impossible. There is no area He can not turn around at any moment. One of the biggest issues we face is not asking God for His divine intervention. When we have confidence in that what we ask according to His word we can have. Read that again! Whatever is in the word of God is available to every believer and that is YOU! What do you want God to do in your situation? This week ASK! God favors you. Your enemies tried but they couldn't triumph over you. ASK ... Lord I need_____ Father I desire _____ Help me _____

Another fear is that God doesn't hear me or He won't because I have messed up in the past. Your past doesn't define your future. Underline that one. It's time to believe again. Believe what God said in His word. He stands behind every promise. Wait for it. Lean on Him. Speak life. Speak prosperity. God's ear is bent toward you, waiting for you to say the same thing He has said. Are you blessed? Were you designed to be a blessing? Do you want to give at another level? Do you want to get out of debt? Do you want to see clearly the systems of the world that are destroying your joy? Is there some family member that is coming against your financial situation? Do you need to be more productive? Is there a financial matter that weighs heavy on your heart? ... ANYTHING ... Just ASK!

Call unto the Lord and watch Him work this week. If you call Him you should be confident knowing that He is faithful to perform all that He said He would. If it is in His word... It's yours!

He is the the first and the last, Whatever you need just ask!

Divinely Connected: Steps to Fearless Financial Freedom

1 Goal for the Week

Date: __/__/____

Scripture/ Affirmation:

TOP 3 TASKS

- ○ _____
- ○ _____
- ○ _____

OTHER TO-DOS:

NOTES:

Mindset _____

Goals _____

Budget _____

Spending _____

Eliminate _____

Automate _____

Debt _____

Credit _____

Giving _____

Savings _____

Investing _____

Business _____

Relationships _____

Family _____

Self Care _____

Divinely Connected: Steps to Fearless Financial Freedom

James 1:17 "Every generous act and every perfect gift is from above, coming down from the Father of lights; with Him there is no variation or shadow cast by turning."

Generosity is the character of our creator. Giving is what He does best; love, peace and don't forget mercy. If you want to be more like your Father in heaven, then giving should be in your nature too.

In order to be generous, we start with a grateful heart. This week add writing a gratitude journal to your TO-DO list (you can use the NOTES section). Get beyond the 'He woke me up this morning and started me on my way'. Yes, God gives us new mercy everyday but what do you have that you are grateful for? Dirty dishes because your family was fed. Tons of clean clothes to fold because you have more than enough to wear. Who has God used as a resource for you to have the provision? God saw the best in you when everyone else around could only see the worst! Who can you turn your attention to and show the love of God? Pour into their best.

Every good gift is from God. List all the good gifts God has given you and lift your hands in worship. Thank Him for all the blessed benefits He has bestowed upon you. When you take time to meditate on God's goodness not only do you acknowledge Him but you are more willing to be a blessing. In your budget this week, evaluate whether you have designed it so that you can be a blessing to others. Is there margin in your finances? Are you taking care of yourself? Self care is important! You are God's child and He wants you to be blessed too. Add a small celebration for just you. You work hard and without the celebration you may become angry and resentful.

Attitudes toward being generous can be changed with the help of God. Declare I need thee, Oh I need thee, every hour I need thee. Let God direct you to make the changes necessary in your budget this week.

Divinely Connected: Steps to Fearless Financial Freedom

1 Goal for the Week

Date: __/__/____

Scripture/ Affirmation:

TOP 3 TASKS

- _____
- _____
- _____

OTHER TO-DOS:

NOTES:

Mindset _____

Goals _____

Budget _____

Spending _____

Eliminate _____

Automate _____

Debt _____

Credit _____

Giving _____

Savings _____

Investing _____

Business _____

Relationships _____

Family _____

Self Care _____

Colossians 3:23-24 "Whatever you do, do it enthusiastically, as something done for the Lord and not for men, knowing that you will receive the reward of an inheritance from the Lord. You serve the Lord Christ."

Serving God is a privilege. Sometimes we overlook the blessing of being allowed to serve. We forget that all that we do should be done for His glory. He will make sure it works out for our good. So do it! Whatever you do… get to work doing and give it everything you've got. Take a look at what you are doing. Is it profitable? Effective? Does it work toward your goals? Is it helpful to others? Is it building the Kingdom?

This week concentrate on eliminating what is bringing you down. Is it that you don't use credit wisely? Are your bills always being paid late and you need to automate? Are you giving too much to others trying to please them?

Our validation comes from God! If we look to Him as our source and our Creator then what He says about us is what matters. Can God brag on you in the area of money management? If not then it's time to make a declaration today that from this day forward it will be different. Lord, just be pleased with our stewardship. Do you hear voices in your head that keep telling you that you are not enough? Replace them by allowing God to pour into you. Take time to put on the helmet of salvation. Remind yourself that you are the righteousness of God in Christ. You are an ambassador of Christ. You are to show forth the praises of Him that has called you out of darkness and into His marvelous light.

God is a rewarder and your reward is waiting! He is a good God, a great God. He is the one that will send a reward. Look for it this week from unexpected places. Then smile and jot it down in your gratitude journal. He is blessing you right now… turn around… there He goes again.

Divinely Connected: Steps to Fearless Financial Freedom

1 Goal for the Week

Date: __/__/____

Scripture/ Affirmation:

TOP 3 TASKS

- _____
- _____
- _____

OTHER TO-DOS:

NOTES:

Mindset _____

Goals _____

Budget _____

Spending _____

Eliminate _____

Automate _____

Debt _____

Credit _____

Giving _____

Savings _____

Investing _____

Business _____

Relationships _____

Family _____

Self Care _____

Divinely Connected: Steps to Fearless Financial Freedom

Ephesians 1:3 "Praise the God and Father of our Lord Jesus Christ, who has blessed us in Christ with every spiritual blessing in the heavens."

You are blessed! You have been blessed with every spiritual blessing! God did that for YOU! Gratitude journal time again. What are the blessings that you acknowledge? Take a moment to praise God for being a great and marvelous God!

Recognizing our blessings makes the journey to fixing our finances easier. Though we haven't arrived, there is light at the end of the tunnel and you aren't traveling alone.

Imagine you taking the journey to debt freedom. It starts out very dark. Feels overwhelming, possibly like drowning. Keep treading water. One step at a time, one payment at a time. Make sure that payment is not just the minimum. If it is only an extra $5 it is moving you closer to the day when you can say you are completely debt free. So for now you are in the deep, out to sea. With each wave you find yourself drifting toward the shore. You keep getting closer as long as you are not accumulating any additional debt. As the shoreline gets closer it builds your anticipation that you will soon be able to stand. As the excitement continues to build your focus turns to a renewed faith and hope that you didn't think was possible but now it's within your grasp. A few more crashes of the waves (monthly payment) and now you stand. Ready to walk to the shore of freedom? It's waiting for you!

This week tally all of your debt. Identify the interest rates, minimum payment and total due. Then use the debt calculator and determine what date you will be debt free! DEBT FREE!!

God release your rain! Pour it out on us that we feel your blessings overtake us. Every extra blessing this week, attack the debt. Watch God work it out!

https://www.vertex42.com/Calculators/debt-reduction-calculator.html

Divinely Connected: Steps to Fearless Financial Freedom

1 Goal for the Week

Date: __/__/____

Scripture/ Affirmation:

TOP 3 TASKS

- ○ _____
- ○ _____
- ○ _____

OTHER TO-DOS:

NOTES:

Mindset _____

Goals _____

Budget _____

Spending _____

Eliminate _____

Automate _____

Debt _____

Credit _____

Giving _____

Savings _____

Investing _____

Business _____

Relationships _____

Family _____

Self Care _____

Divinely Connected: Steps to Fearless Financial Freedom

Proverbs 10:22 "The Lord's blessing enriches, and struggle adds nothing to it."

The blessing of the Lord comes with no struggle! That is great news. The struggles that we face then is a result of our handiwork. We are frustrated when we add our works of the flesh. So let's decide this week not to add struggle but to concentrate on the Holy Spirit's leading.

It's already done! God continues to bless you. Look through the income portion of your budget. How much more can God bless you? Are you acknowledging Him each day for what He has already given? Every time you turn around He keeps on blessing you. He comes through!

Deciding not to struggle sounds good on paper but can be difficult if you are a planner and you keep revolving over and over in your mind trying to figure a way out. This week, put it down on paper what you need and ask God to bless. Set your budget... balanced or not. Ask God to lead you to the areas that need your attention. Don't grapple with what to do. Set it down for 5 minutes and wait for God to show you. Then just do it! Take action. Remove the dining out line item in your budget. You can cook at home, make your lunch, and give up that coffee you buy. Now be grateful that God showed you some of the waste. It may only be for a season.

Let's revisit the blessings that God has given that have no strings attached. No additional debt. No struggle. The Lord should be praised for graciously providing and protecting you especially when human effort has reached its limit. Take the shackles off your feet and dance! Dance before the Lord about all the many blessings He has bestowed. Praise Him now for being so good.

Just Praise Him!

Divinely Connected: Steps to Fearless Financial Freedom

 # 1 Goal for the Week

Date: __/__/____

Scripture/ Affirmation:

TOP 3 TASKS

- _____
- _____
- _____

OTHER TO-DOS:

NOTES:

Mindset _____

Goals _____

Budget _____

Spending _____

Eliminate _____

Automate _____

Debt _____

Credit _____

Giving _____

Savings _____

Investing _____

Business _____

Relationships _____

Family _____

Self Care _____

Divinely Connected: Steps to Fearless Financial Freedom

2 Peter 1:2-3 "May grace and peace be multiplied to you through the knowledge of God and of Jesus our Lord. His divine power has given us everything required for life and godliness through the knowledge of Him who called us by His glory and goodness."

God's divine power gives us everything! Divine power!! That means that no matter what you are up against, the power of God can break it. Watch God change it! Oh my... God is more than able! And He gives us everything we need.

This life has its challenges we all admit. Sometimes overwhelmed is how we feel but that's an inward focus. Changing that focus to see the God of all glory as greater than anything we face allows us to view the small situation like David. Who or what is that supposed giant in relation to the God that we serve? He says everything pertaining to life is already given to us. So, count on it!

God's grace keeps following you. That means that there is so much favor on your life that others see it. You are a walking anointing. What seems difficult for others to manage, you do with ease. What would cause others to stress and be in a straight jacket, you walk in peace. There is a smile on your face regardless of the storms that are raging. You battle the angry seas not by yourself, but with the help of God. He graced YOU! You don't look like what you've been through! And if you did that my sister/brother, what prevents you from handling the current trial the same way. It's time for God to intervene and you to rest in Him.

God's grace and peace will be multiplied to you through the knowledge of Him. So go get that knowledge! This week, spend time getting to know God better. Discover something new about His character and emulate that in your life. Let it be seen in your money management skills. Does He count the cost first? Is He generous? Does He prioritize the Kingdom? Does He bless you to be a blessing? Yes, God is strategic, generous, intentional and empowering. Now go out and do the same!

Divinely Connected: Steps to Fearless Financial Freedom

1 Goal for the Week

Date: __/__/____

Scripture/ Affirmation:

TOP 3 TASKS

- _____
- _____
- _____

OTHER TO-DOS:

NOTES:

Mindset _____

Goals _____

Budget _____

Spending _____

Eliminate _____

Automate _____

Debt _____

Credit _____

Giving _____

Savings _____

Investing _____

Business _____

Relationships _____

Family _____

Self Care _____

Divinely Connected: Steps to Fearless Financial Freedom

John 15:10 "If you keep My commands you will remain in My love, just as I have kept My Father's commands and remain in His love."

Keeping God's commands is easy If we agree with them. It's when those commands irritate our flesh that we start looking sideways at the pages of the holy book. Yet, the promise is sure. Obey and you will be blessed!

If we keep God's commands, we remain. We dwell in His presence and experience His love. What does love do? It covers, it protects, it provides and it gives! God is great! And greatly to be praised. The love that He shows is unconditional. If you want to abide in His love then His commands and statues are to be followed. So, what must we do?

Tithing is a taboo subject to some. Let's look at it this way, to be in covenant relationship with God, we should acknowledge Him. This means we recognize that He is the giver of everything. It all belongs to Him and He alone gives us the power to do what we do. Our income is wholly because of Him. He woke us up. He gives us breath and brains. He affords us activity of our limbs and therefore the ability to move and do what is necessary to earn a living. Now this income gives us the privilege to give back. The first 10% belongs to God in acknowledgment of who He is and what He has done. Can you give more? Of course! The tithe or first 10th is what God asks for in response to His love. This week commit to returning the tithe and be consistent with it. As soon as you receive, give.

This may bring up the subject of budgeting again. Yes, your tithe should be automatically included in your budget. So should your savings. If you plan your budget to be no more than 80% of your income, you will have the makings of acknowledging God and becoming an automatic millionaire. Are you ready?

10% Tithe and 10% Savings... that's your challenge for the week. Let's go forth and prosper!

Divinely Connected: Steps to Fearless Financial Freedom

1 Goal for the Week

Date: __/__/____

Scripture/ Affirmation:

TOP 3 TASKS

- _____
- _____
- _____

OTHER TO-DOS:

NOTES:

Mindset _____

Goals _____

Budget _____

Spending _____

Eliminate _____

Automate _____

Debt _____

Credit _____

Giving _____

Savings _____

Investing _____

Business _____

Relationships _____

Family _____

Self Care _____

Divinely Connected: Steps to Fearless Financial Freedom

Jeremiah 29:11 "For I know the plans I have for you – this is the Lord's declaration – plans for your welfare, not for disaster, to give you a future and a hope."

When you feel like giving up, this familiar Scripture brings comfort and joy. God has never given up on you! He has great plans for you and they are for His glory and for your good.

So what PLANS could He have for you that you don't see? Purpose! Yes, God has a great purpose for you to accomplish. Before you were formed in your mother's womb, He knew you. Think on the fact that there is a great purpose that God designed you for. Are you walking in it? Do you have any idea what it is? Do your goals reflect that purpose? This week look at the goals you have and align them with the purpose you think God has for you.

Legacy is the "L" in plans. You should be considering what you are going to leave to your children's children. Yes, actual money! Plan ahead and prepare to take care of all your arrangements and your bills. Don't leave it for your children to have to figure it out. That's a motivator to be debt free. Identify a debt reduction goal for this next month.

Activities Is our next step. What are you doing to eliminate debt and automate your bill paying so that your credit score will rise. There are several activities you can do. Get busy this week in your TOP 3 TO-DO items to identify at least 1 that will address this area that will bring you peace.

"N" references your nature. You are uniquely designed and by tapping into those strengths you can remove the struggle in money management. It's called your Biblical Financial Personality. Your mindset and your strengths hold the key to true financial freedom. God designed you that way for a reason and He has equipped you to walk in it. It's time to embrace your uniqueness!

The final letter represents the Systems. The world system is set to have you struggle and put you in bondage. It's time to be released! Meditate on the fact that God's plan isn't for you to be conformed to the world but to be transformed. He hasn't set you up for disaster but for a future and a hope. Envision your future! Dream big! Hope! Expect something good to happen this week.

Divinely Connected: Steps to Fearless Financial Freedom

 # 1 Goal for the Week

Date: __/__/____

Scripture/ Affirmation:

TOP 3 TASKS
- ○ _____
- ○ _____
- ○ _____

OTHER TO-DOS:

NOTES:

Mindset _____

Goals _____

Budget _____

Spending _____

Eliminate _____

Automate _____

Debt _____

Credit _____

Giving _____

Savings _____

Investing _____

Business _____

Relationships _____

Family _____

Self Care _____

Philippians 4:12 "I know how to have a little, and I know how to have a lot. In any and all circumstances I have learned the secret of being content – whether well fed or hungry, whether in abundance or in need."

Learning to be content is an ability to completely rely upon God and recognize that He knows best. Our dependence on God and His resources removes the struggle from us having to make things work.

Learning to have little and being content is equivalent to your current circumstance. Do you see the blessing in what you have? Do you see how God makes a way? Miracles happen in your life daily all because God knows your situation and cares so much about you! On your way to where God wants to take you there is a key to getting there. The key is to praise God where you are! Take a moment to bless His holy name for all that He has done already. Don't ask for anything just worship Him as Lord and King. He has been so good. Review your entire budget and thank God that He is faithful.

The focus for this passage is on your attitude toward what God has given you. No comparing yourself to where someone else has moved. Be grateful for what God has given to you. Seek His face and not His hand.

If you find yourself abundantly blessed, how has your attitude changed? God loves a humble spirit... He resists the proud and gives grace to the humble. It takes more work to remain in a posture of gratitude to God when you have amassed plenty. It's time to check your attitude toward others. When it comes to abounding, are you still laying before the feet of Jesus? You are blessed to be a blessing. Make sure your budget reflects the blessing that you are designed to be... Praise Him again!

Divinely Connected: Steps to Fearless Financial Freedom

1 Goal for the Week

Date: __/__/____

Scripture/ Affirmation:

TOP 3 TASKS

- _____
- _____
- _____

OTHER TO-DOS:

NOTES:

Mindset _____

Goals _____

Budget _____

Spending _____

Eliminate _____

Automate _____

Debt _____

Credit _____

Giving _____

Savings _____

Investing _____

Business _____

Relationships _____

Family _____

Self Care _____

Divinely Connected: Steps to Fearless Financial Freedom

2 Thessalonians 3:10b-11 "'If anyone isn't willing to work, he should not eat.' For we hear that there are some among you who walk irresponsibly, not working at all, but interfering with the work of others."

The willingness to work, the attitude to participate in your own deliverance from financial struggle is the issue. God designed you with a purpose. You are to be a blessing to others and not a burden. We cripple ourselves when we adopt a victim mentality and look for others to provide for us rather than relying on God and His giftings.

Our heavenly Father provides for us in a multitude of ways. He gives us life and the abilities to live that life in abundance. The abilities God has bestowed upon you should be used to increase your income. Are you utilizing all that God has gifted you with? Do you have passive income? (Income that doesn't rely on you working another day or hour) Have you positioned yourself to continue increasing your income? Are you doing excellent work as unto the Lord?

If you have been complacent in the past, now is the time to repent and ask God for a new attitude. Surrender! It's time to stand before God arms wide open. How can God bless a stationary ship. You are a yacht designed to sail the amazing seas! Don't settle for only being in a pond that isn't equipped to allow you to dock. It's time to change your perspective. Nothing worthwhile will be handed to you. It's time to go forth and walk in abundance. Push through complacency into competence. You got this because you are already equipped so now be empowered. Sit in God's presence and receive the restoration and encouragement to do all that He has designed for you.

This week look for opportunities that you may have missed to increase your income without extra effort. Ask God to show you what you are working with and where to apply yourself. Then either craft something new or tweak what you have started. Now is the time to ask for strategy to implement what God has shown.

Divinely Connected: Steps to Fearless Financial Freedom

Date: __/__/____

 # 1 Goal for the Week

Scripture/ Affirmation:

TOP 3 TASKS

- ○ _____
- ○ _____
- ○ _____

OTHER TO-DOS: NOTES:

Mindset _____

Goals _____

Budget _____

Spending _____

Eliminate _____

Automate _____

Debt _____

Credit _____

Giving _____

Savings _____

Investing _____

Business _____

Relationships _____

Family _____

Self Care _____

Divinely Connected: Steps to Fearless Financial Freedom

Deuteronomy 8:17-18 "You may say to yourself 'My power and my own ability have gained this wealth for me,' but remember that the Lord your God gives you the power to gain wealth, in order to confirm His covenant He swore to your fathers, as it is today."

Have you ever blessed someone by taking care of a financial situation they put themselves in, only for them to forget you and your help? They walk away after taking all that you have without more than a simple thank you. The natural tendency would be to never provide assistance to them again. It hurts to give and sometimes sacrifice to provide relief for others only to be forgotten.

God gave ALL for us. He sacrificed and yet often He is forgotten when we look at money. Why are there any areas in life that we keep God from intervening in to help us improve? Stewardship recognizes that we are just managers of the funds that belong to God. He gave us what we have to enjoy and to bless. Our relationship with God affords us access and should also urge us to give Him access in response. Relationship is a two-way street. God gives and we return. Money talks and it does have a lot to say about us! Make sure it is speaking very highly of you and the God that you serve!

Our abilities come from God so it seems reasonable that we acknowledge that it is He that gives us the power to get wealth. That power is the authority and the ability to gain. The authority says that as a child of God you have been graced with gifts to perform. Walk in the abilities God has blessed you with. Don't sit on your gift! If your haters or frienemies are jealous, be understanding but don't stop moving! You have been endowed with heaven's blessings so use them. Give yourself permission to prosper.

God wants you to prosper or He wouldn't have empowered you to do so!

Divinely Connected: Steps to Fearless Financial Freedom

1 Goal for the Week

Date: __/__/____

Scripture/ Affirmation:

TOP 3 TASKS

- ○ _____
- ○ _____
- ○ _____

OTHER TO-DOS:

NOTES:

Mindset _____

Goals _____

Budget _____

Spending _____

Eliminate _____

Automate _____

Debt _____

Credit _____

Giving _____

Savings _____

Investing _____

Business _____

Relationships _____

Family _____

Self Care _____

Psalm 37:21 "The wicked man borrows and does not repay, but the righteous one is gracious and giving."

Having the character of the One who loves you and sacrificed for you is the ultimate goal. Recognizing that you are the righteousness of God in Christ Jesus means accepting responsibility for our past decisions. You bought it, now pay for it is the strong command.

You just can't give up now. Nobody told you the road would be easy but I don't believe He brought you this far to leave you. No one said it would be easy. You have come to far from where you started. If you believe that God believes in you then also believe in yourself. Let's make a plan and get this done!

This week is about debt reduction. List all of your debts. Don't leave out the family member you owe. List them in order of your borrowing if it is a person. List them in order of lowest to highest for revolving accounts. Make sure you identify who you owe, how much you owe (balance), how much you pay monthly (minimum requirement), and the interest rate. Now breath…

There are different methods to attack your debt. The snowball method encourages you to pay off the smallest one first. Once you've paid the first one off, use that minimum to add to the minimum of the next one on the list. This way you gain momentum and are encouraged that you can eliminate your debt. The avalanche method reorders the debt from the highest interest to the lowest. When you pay off the highest interest rate card or loan first, you pay the least amount of interest overall. You may not have the immediate gratification of eliminating a debt but you've saved in the long run.

This week make a plan to pay what you owe. Write out your goal. Don't feel condemned by your past decisions, just make better ones going forward. Then thank Jesus, mercy said NO! His mercy is new everyday!

Divinely Connected: Steps to Fearless Financial Freedom

1 Goal for the Week

Date: __/__/____

Scripture/ Affirmation:

TOP 3 TASKS
- _____
- _____
- _____

OTHER TO-DOS: **NOTES:**

Mindset _____

Goals _____

Budget _____

Spending _____

Eliminate _____

Automate _____

Debt _____

Credit _____

Giving _____

Savings _____

Investing _____

Business _____

Relationships _____

Family _____

Self Care _____

Psalm 112:1-3 "Hallelujah! Happy is the man who fears the Lord, taking great delight in His commands. His descendants will be powerful in the land; the generation of the upright will be blessed. Wealth and riches are in his house, and his righteousness endures forever."

Taking delight in the commands of God is a prerequisite to having wealth and riches in your house. God's divine wisdom is what allows us to prosper. Commands that discourage co-signing and encourages gaining interest and income are wise counsel for the one who listens. Any student of the Word knows that God's desire is for us to prosper. His commands propel us to make prosperity come to fruition.

The past is not an indicator of the future. Decisions made without consulting God may have led to bad judgement and consequences but it doesn't mean that you have to stay there. Hear God, when you abide in His word you will know the truth. When you apply His word, all grace abounds. That means you get what you didn't deserve and you should look for miracles around every corner.

This week look for the miracles as you apply His commands. Is there an area you are really searching for answers? Look in the Bible for scriptural references that address your situation. If you have too much debt, discover the causes of debt. If you don't have enough income, focus on the giftings of God that will help you see yourself like God sees you. If you aren't motivated to work, read about laziness. If you aren't satisfied with what you have and aren't grateful, concentrate on contentment.

God has a great plan for you. His word gives commands that if you follow will reap benefits both now and in the future.

Divinely Connected: Steps to Fearless Financial Freedom

1 Goal for the Week

Date: __/__/____

Scripture/ Affirmation:

TOP 3 TASKS

- ○ _____
- ○ _____
- ○ _____

OTHER TO-DOS:

NOTES:

Mindset _____

Goals _____

Budget _____

Spending _____

Eliminate _____

Automate _____

Debt _____

Credit _____

Giving _____

Savings _____

Investing _____

Business _____

Relationships _____

Family _____

Self Care _____

Divinely Connected: Steps to Fearless Financial Freedom

Read Matthew 20:1-16

Comparison almost always brings disillusionment. We know we are worth more but don't know how to quantify it. We see others getting ahead and know we have put in much more than they and we get depressed. Looking to the side at what someone else is doing and comparing it to oneself is the fastest way to start a pity party. Jealousy isn't of God and neither is covetousness. Going down this road...No one wins.

Instead of looking horizontally at what someone else does, look vertically and ask God to take care of you. When you ask God what He thinks, the conversation changes to gratitude.

Are you grateful for your pay? Are you thankful for the opportunity to work? So many don't have the privileges of the job you have. Write a list of all the benefits that aren't in your paycheck; include company car, trips, vacations, sick days, etc. Write a gratitude list of all the contacts you have because of where you work. Your paycheck is only a portion of what you are gaining. If you had more responsibility you would also have less time to spend with family and friends. There may be some other concessions you would have to make.

This week be grateful and count your blessings. You'll begin to see all the things that the Lord has done.

Now don't stop with the gratitude, ASK God for more if that's your desire. The Bible says you have not because you ask not. Go ahead and dream big. Write a list of what you would like God to do for you. Make it specific. Can you write out 100 things? 300? Make it a long list. Now read the list morning and night. When God accomplishes it, check it off. In a year, you will have a praise like no other. Thank God in advance for the mighty works of His hands!

Divinely Connected: Steps to Fearless Financial Freedom

1 Goal for the Week

Date: __/__/____

Scripture/ Affirmation:

TOP 3 TASKS

- _____
- _____
- _____

OTHER TO-DOS: **NOTES:**

Mindset _____

Goals _____

Budget _____

Spending _____

Eliminate _____

Automate _____

Debt _____

Credit _____

Giving _____

Savings _____

Investing _____

Business _____

Relationships _____

Family _____

Self Care _____

Divinely Connected: Steps to Fearless Financial Freedom

Read Luke 12:16-21

Imagine you have two accounts. One account you are constantly pouring into. The other account you leave empty. You always plan to put something in the empty account but your focus is on the one for yourself.

This passage reminds us that there is a heavenly account and an earthly account. If we focus so much on building up the earthly account that we are selfish (only looking out for our own interests), where will it go? We can't take money with us when we die. Have you ever seen a Brink's truck in a funeral procession? If the account marked heaven is depleted or empty we are the losers on so many levels.

God has done so much for us. We think of the life He gives and the giftings He endows. We recognize that it is His plan for our lives and His favor that He bestows on us. Why then would we think that our heavenly account should be overlooked for our earthly one? If we pray asking God to bless us, what if the request came back insufficient funds? If there is nothing in the account, we have nothing to draw from.

This week evaluate your giving. All of your giving should be taken into account. Yes, tithing should be your minimum standard of giving but offerings should also be done. The tithe goes to your local assembly where you are fed the word of God. Offerings can go there or to other ministries. Balance your budget where you have the ability to give to others as well. If someone is in need of a meal, or you see someone on the street, build in a margin so you have something to bless them with.

God created you not only to be blessed, but to be a blessing.

Divinely Connected: Steps to Fearless Financial Freedom

1 Goal for the Week

Date: __/__/____

Scripture/ Affirmation:

TOP 3 TASKS

- _____
- _____
- _____

OTHER TO-DOS:

NOTES:

Mindset _____

Goals _____

Budget _____

Spending _____

Eliminate _____

Automate _____

Debt _____

Credit _____

Giving _____

Savings _____

Investing _____

Business _____

Relationships _____

Family _____

Self Care _____

James 2:15-17 "If a brother or sister is without clothes and lacks daily food and one of you says to them, 'Go in peace, keep warm, and eat well,' but you don't give them what the body needs, what good is it? In the same way faith, if it doesn't have works, is dead by itself."

Having something to bless someone with is a way that our faith is moved into action. God desires that we bless others. There are those in need that are looking for your light to shine. You are commanded to do good works so that they may acknowledge God.

Riding down the street in some major cities we can be accosted by those that are homeless. The strangers and the orphans in the Old Testament were taken care of by the offerings. God's character is shown in how He treated and prepared for them. Your representation of God is then shown in how you treat others. Is it a requirement to always give to those who ask? Tough question. The Bible does tell us to be ready to assist but wisdom prevails in a perverse generation. There are con-artists that prey on good people. Wisdom says be ready to give but ask the Holy Spirit for direction.

As you contemplate this passage, see God. He says faith without corresponding action is dead faith. How can you trust in God and not have the works to go with it? Can you say that you have God's compassion but not go visit the sick? Can you say you are concerned about the lost and not evangelize? Can you say that you love God whom you can not see but hate your brother that you can see?

This week be grateful but give someone a reason to acknowledge God. Pay it forward for what He has done for you. Pick up someone's tab. Buy a meal for a homeless person on the street. If they weren't honest, don't worry God won't be mad that you blessed them anyway.

Divinely Connected: Steps to Fearless Financial Freedom

 # 1 Goal for the Week

Date: __/__/____

Scripture/ Affirmation:

TOP 3 TASKS

- _____
- _____
- _____

OTHER TO-DOS:

NOTES:

Mindset _____

Goals _____

Budget _____

Spending _____

Eliminate _____

Automate _____

Debt _____

Credit _____

Giving _____

Savings _____

Investing _____

Business _____

Relationships _____

Family _____

Self Care _____

Divinely Connected: Steps to Fearless Financial Freedom

Acts 2:44-47 "Now all the believers were together and held all things in common... distributed... as anyone had need... they ate their food with a joyful and humble attitude, praising God and having favor with all the people..."

It's easy to say there was a time when we held all things in common and wish that others would meet our every need. As the church began, there was a coming out of one system and moving to a different way of thinking. The change in thinking is one of family. We are in the Kingdom and our Kingdom mindset is one of being other centered.

God's desire is for us to look out for our brothers and sisters in Christ. Several passages come to mind that encourage us to not focus inward but to consider others in preference to ourselves. Does that mean you aren't important? Of course not. God so values you and the contribution He desires for you to make in this world. Love your neighbor as you love yourself!

You were created for such a time as this. You have so much to give for the benefit of others. Each of us in Christ is to help the other rise above. Remember, we overcome by the blood of the Lamb and the word of our testimony. This week let's do some testifying. Be a blessing and pay it forward. You don't know how you can put a smile on someone's face or better yet be the miracle they have been praying for! Let's walk in victory together!

So how does this passage instruct us this week? Having an other focused outlook encourages gift giving, offering and consideration of what others may deal with. Check your budget for holes in giving. There should be three buckets that all of your money goes into: spending, saving and giving. If you have too much in the spending – cut back. If you have nothing in the saving or giving – add a line item and recalculate.

Divinely Connected: Steps to Fearless Financial Freedom

1 Goal for the Week

Date: __/__/____

Scripture/ Affirmation:

TOP 3 TASKS

- ○ _____
- ○ _____
- ○ _____

OTHER TO-DOS: **NOTES:**

Mindset _____

Goals _____

Budget _____

Spending _____

Eliminate _____

Automate _____

Debt _____

Credit _____

Giving _____

Savings _____

Investing _____

Business _____

Relationships _____

Family _____

Self Care _____

Divinely Connected: Steps to Fearless Financial Freedom

Matthew 6:19-21 "Don't collect for yourselves treasure on earth… but collect for yourselves treasures in heaven… For where your treasure is, there your heart will be also."

Imagine you are going on a treasure hunt. You have the map to get there and the anticipation that it will be worth your time. You eagerly go from place to place meticulously following the map. When you arrive at the X that marks the spot of the treasure you find a extra large chest. You take a deep breath as you open it… only to find that it's not what you expected. You find the remnants of valuable objects destroyed by time. So it goes with earthly possessions.

You are God's treasure. You are valuable to the Kingdom. There is no earthly replacement for you. Recognize that your influence and impact has been preordained by God. He has the oceans, sky and rainbows yet created you to add to His majestic creations. You are the ultimate treasure! Relationship with you is the desire of the Creator of the universe. A little lower than the angels and crowned with glory and honor, that's you! Now go and allow someone to find the treasure inside of you… be a blessing.

Switch your focus to the things you keep and prize. Where are they stored? Are they earthly things that you can't take with you. Will they be outdated and old news in a few months? Are they really that valuable?

We are admonished to check our heart. Our heart or passions go where we focus our attention and store in that treasure chest what we deem important. This week look at your priorities. Check your bank account debits. Are you spending more on the superficial things that will get holes in them or are soon outdated? Are you more focused on heavenly things and putting money where your hearts' desires are located?

God of all creation, show us the importance of Kingdom investments.

Divinely Connected: Steps to Fearless Financial Freedom

1 Goal for the Week

Date: __/__/____

Scripture/ Affirmation:

TOP 3 TASKS

- ○ _____
- ○ _____
- ○ _____

OTHER TO-DOS:

NOTES:

Mindset _____

Goals _____

Budget _____

Spending _____

Eliminate _____

Automate _____

Debt _____

Credit _____

Giving _____

Savings _____

Investing _____

Business _____

Relationships _____

Family _____

Self Care _____

Divinely Connected: Steps to Fearless Financial Freedom

Romans 12:2 "Do not be conformed to this age, but be transformed by the renewing of your mind, so that you may discern what is the good, pleasing and perfect will of God."

Needing the leading of the Holy Spirit is a blessing and necessary to overcome the systems of the world. God's ways are different in nature and outcome than the worlds. The true and living God is master of everything and He gives us the benefit of that wisdom. You have been given the key to prosperity. Let's change our minds!

Our thinking is what either elevates us to a Kingdom mindset or condemns us to shackles of the bondage of the world. How is your thinking? Have you bought into the systems? Do you consider yourself a victim? Do you always have an excuse of why you don't achieve or accumulate wealth? Is it someone else's fault that you aren't further along? Do you think someone owes you?

God has created you special! There is no one like you and there never will be! Yes, you may have had a few bad days and some trauma. They don't define who you are nor do they limit your ability. If on the inside of you there is the power of God residing, then tell me who and what can hinder you? Greater is He that is in you than he that is in the world! You have power dwelling inside that hasn't been tapped. It's time to release that power!

This week work on your mindset. Think the way God thinks. As you study this week consider what God says about you and also about what He wants for you. His desire is that you prosper! Anything that goes against you prospering in season and out of season is not God's plan. Identify those areas – debt, bad decisions, condemning thoughts, dream killers, etc. – and write a Scripture to counter the thought or system.

Decide today to think like God and rely on the Holy Spirit to lead you. And when He does... follow!

Divinely Connected: Steps to Fearless Financial Freedom

 # 1 Goal for the Week

Date: __/__/____

Scripture/ Affirmation:

TOP 3 TASKS

- _____
- _____
- _____

OTHER TO-DOS:

NOTES:

Mindset _____

Goals _____

Budget _____

Spending _____

Eliminate _____

Automate _____

Debt _____

Credit _____

Giving _____

Savings _____

Investing _____

Business _____

Relationships _____

Family _____

Self Care _____

Divinely Connected: Steps to Fearless Financial Freedom

Mark 14:7 "You always have the poor with you, and you can do what is good for them whenever you want, but you do not always have Me."

Every praise is due our God. Every word of worship with one accord. Every praise is to our God! Thank Him for the blessed benefits He has given you.

Poor can be used to define a destitute state physically, mentally, emotionally and/or financially. If that doesn't identify you, then give God praise! Being without what we desire is not depleted of resources. Having little but having some is an opportunity to focus on the positive and not dwell on the lack.

The cattle on a thousand hills belongs to God. With Him there is nothing that is impossible. So asking for our needs is in order. However, when we encounter those that have less than we do, it is an opportunity to be the blessing. You have the ability to meet needs. What good do you want to do for the poor? What brings your heart joy in helping or serving others? Can you realign your budget to be able to give where your heart desires?

The benefit of giving to met others needs is that we develop the heart of God! His DNA is evident in our lives. We become light for those in darkness. Yield to the desires that God has placed in you. Stand before the King and praise Him for all that He has done for you. Look back over your life and thank Him.

This week review your past monthly budgets. Are there areas that need your attention? Is there something you can automate so that it doesn't get by you again? Is there a ministry you want to give to consistently? Are there bills you want to schedule to improve your credit score? This week the word is automate!

Divinely Connected: Steps to Fearless Financial Freedom

1 Goal for the Week

Date: __/__/____

Scripture/ Affirmation:

TOP 3 TASKS

- ○ _____
- ○ _____
- ○ _____

OTHER TO-DOS:

NOTES:

Mindset _____

Goals _____

Budget _____

Spending _____

Eliminate _____

Automate _____

Debt _____

Credit _____

Giving _____

Savings _____

Investing _____

Business _____

Relationships _____

Family _____

Self Care _____

1 Timothy 5:8 "But if anyone does not provide for his own, that is his own household, he has denied the faith and is worse than an unbeliever."

Family is the nucleus of our relationships. It is the backbone that formed us and the launch pad from which we leap. Our molding starts with the foundation given us by those to whom we were entrusted. Does that mean that our families are perfect? By no stretch of the imagination. You may even think that yours downright stinks. Our family dynamics molds us into who we are... we take the good with the bad. We learn from them what to do and what not to do. We then are launched into the world to make a path and bring others along.

Our God pours much into each family. The mother that nurtures and the grandmother that prays is not without the help of God. The father that provides and protects and the grandfather that teaches lessons of old wrapped in wisdom is from God too. When we consider that our Heavenly Father teaches us many lessons through our first teachers, we are beholden to them for being the vessels through which we have come to this point.

Are your parents aging? Is there a family member that needs your assistance? The urging here is to see through the eyes of God and to make sure you provide for those who provided for you. Is there wiggle room in your budget to do something nice for Mom? If one needs long term care soon, have you prepared for that? Make sure it is in the forefront of your mind to take care of those that took care of you. It doesn't matter if it was what you wanted. Consider that they did the best they could with what they knew to do. Show mercy! And then sprinkle it with a little grace! You too may pass this way.

Divinely Connected: Steps to Fearless Financial Freedom

Date: __/__/____

1 Goal for the Week

Scripture/ Affirmation:

TOP 3 TASKS

- _____
- _____
- _____

OTHER TO-DOS:

NOTES:

Mindset _____

Goals _____

Budget _____

Spending _____

Eliminate _____

Automate _____

Debt _____

Credit _____

Giving _____

Savings _____

Investing _____

Business _____

Relationships _____

Family _____

Self Care _____

Luke 12:48 "...Much will be required of everyone who has been given much. And even more will be expected of the one who has been entrusted with more."

Even more Lord! Thank you for even more! To whom much is given, much is required! You probably grew up hearing that often. But have you considered the 'much' you have been given?

We have life itself! Thank you Lord for entrusting us to be here at this time. There is much to be done and many to influence. Thank you Lord for our families! You have blessed us to be in community that pours love into us. As we pour out that love, we see the value and the treasure of being connected. We have clothes to wear and shoes on our feet! God we bless you that we aren't naked. Oh the thought of not being covered, ugh! Jobs, houses, investments, children... the list goes on. Write that list this week and take the time to praise God for each and every blessing. Can you stand to receive much more? Then ask for it!

As we consider the much that we have, we also need to contemplate what we are going to do with it. Are you consistently blessing someone else? Are you a generous giver? Is there room for you to wrap your arms around a stranger or a friend? Ask God this week to identify someone who is in need that He wants you to bless. Be led by the Holy Spirit. Walk in the anointing of God and be the miracle that you are looking for.

Divinely Connected: Steps to Fearless Financial Freedom

1 Goal for the Week

Date: __/__/____

Scripture/ Affirmation:

TOP 3 TASKS

- ○ _____
- ○ _____
- ○ _____

OTHER TO-DOS:

NOTES:

Mindset _____

Goals _____

Budget _____

Spending _____

Eliminate _____

Automate _____

Debt _____

Credit _____

Giving _____

Savings _____

Investing _____

Business _____

Relationships _____

Family _____

Self Care _____

Divinely Connected: Steps to Fearless Financial Freedom

James 2:17 "Honor everyone. Love the brotherhood. Fear God. Honor the Emperor."

Attitude is everything. It determines our altitude. How we think, process and perceive determines how high we go and what we accomplish. Lord give us humble spirits to acknowledge you and your creation!

God has created every human, whether we agree with them or not. We are His handiwork. Because we don't know the end from the beginning and can't see where a person will take a turn for the better, our responsibility is to speak life to the good in them. Honor says that we acknowledge the God that created them and allow Him to do the work. Let's not stand in the way of God's working it out for their good and His glory! Give respect and you will be respected in return.

Love the brotherhood! Our brothers and sisters in Christ are to be cherished. In rubbing us the wrong way they help the diamond in us shine through. 'Brother and sister sandpaper' are only instruments in God's hands to improve us. See them as family and show them the love of God.

Our test when it comes to money issues usually boils down to matters of the heart. How do you feel and treat others both in the Kingdom and without? What is your attitude toward God and His commands on money? Do you respect authority? God's authority? Are you honoring God's wishes in your handling of the funds He has entrusted to you?

It's attitude adjustment time. Align your attitude with that of Christ. He sat with those who others rejected because He came to seek and save the lost. He cared deeply for those who followed Him and gave His life for them. He always acknowledged the Father and bent His will to please Him. And Christ respected the law of the land and found a way to transcend what was required. Display Christ!

Divinely Connected: Steps to Fearless Financial Freedom

1 Goal for the Week

Date: __/__/____

Scripture/ Affirmation:

TOP 3 TASKS

- ○ _____
- ○ _____
- ○ _____

OTHER TO-DOS:

NOTES:

Mindset _____

Goals _____

Budget _____

Spending _____

Eliminate _____

Automate _____

Debt _____

Credit _____

Giving _____

Savings _____

Investing _____

Business _____

Relationships _____

Family _____

Self Care _____

Divinely Connected: Steps to Fearless Financial Freedom

1 Timothy 6:17 "Instruct those who are rich in the present age not to be arrogant or to set their hope on the uncertainty of wealth, but on God, who richly provides us with all things to enjoy."

Lord, help us not to be arrogant! Help us not to think more highly of ourselves than we ought to! God is the one who gives us the power to get wealth. When we confuse the blessings as something we attained by our own power, we are in danger of losing it. The uncertainty that came with the pandemic showed the placement of trust. If the trust was in the riches, the jobs, others and they weren't able to provide, the ground beneath our feet became shaky. Money is fleeting and the stock market goes up and down. Trusting in any earthly instrument to gain is risky business. It's time to shift our focus.

Trusting in God is a sure bet. He hasn't failed yet. He has a track record of coming through not when you want Him but He is always on time. It may not take the path that you desire but the final destination is always for your good. Focusing our expectation on God and the things He gives us to enjoy reframes the narrative to be positive and grateful not arrogant and boastful. It makes for a better friend.

Stress and anxiety come from worrying about things that we can't control. So instead, focus on the One that control everything! Be anxious for nothing but in everything by prayer and supplication with thanksgiving make your request known. That attitude of thanksgiving is one of gratefulness not based on what you can do but what God is able to do. And He is able!

This week turn your biggest concern over to God and watch Him work. Even when you don't see Him working, even when you can't feel Him working. He never stops working! God's got it!

Divinely Connected: Steps to Fearless Financial Freedom

1 Goal for the Week

_____

Date: __/__/____

Scripture/ Affirmation:

TOP 3 TASKS

- _____
- _____
- _____

OTHER TO-DOS:

NOTES:

Mindset _____

Goals _____

Budget _____

Spending _____

Eliminate _____

Automate _____

Debt _____

Credit _____

Giving _____

Savings _____

Investing _____

Business _____

Relationships _____

Family _____

Self Care _____

1 Timothy 6:6-8 "But godliness with contentment is great gain. For we brought nothing into the world, and we can take nothing out. But if we have food and clothing, we will be content with these."

Gratitude looks good on you! Did you know that your attitude shows on your face? Not only is it a sweet smelling savor in God's nostrils but it is becoming to others.

There is much to be thankful for! God has provided us each day with new mercies, and His grace that is sufficient for whatever comes our way. That relying on Christ's sufficiency is what gives us contentment. Satisfaction in what Christ has provided, will make possible, and is currently prescribing, is the basis of our gratitude list.

God is Almighty, all powerful and all knowing. He sees the end before the beginning and promises greater days are ahead. He knows what we need before we even ask and then He provides. He is faithful and has promised to never leave us nor abandon us. Dependable God is the one we serve! It's good to be a favored child of the King.

What you focus on increases and improves. Let's focus on being grateful and watch those areas increase. We are commanded to write the vision and make it plain. Do just that! Write out the vision you are believing God for… then upgrade it! We serve a God that does exceeding, abundantly, above all that we can ask or think. Think bigger and then write it down.

The gratitude journal that you are developing is also a place to put not only material things but attitude adjustments too. We can't take it with us so let's give generously because we have been given so much.

Divinely Connected: Steps to Fearless Financial Freedom

1 Goal for the Week

Date: __/__/____

Scripture/ Affirmation:

TOP 3 TASKS

- _____
- _____
- _____

OTHER TO-DOS:

NOTES:

Mindset _____

Goals _____

Budget _____

Spending _____

Eliminate _____

Automate _____

Debt _____

Credit _____

Giving _____

Savings _____

Investing _____

Business _____

Relationships _____

Family _____

Self Care _____

Divinely Connected: Steps to Fearless Financial Freedom

Matthew 25:14-30 "…turned over his possessions to them… each according to his own ability… Well done… You were faithful over a few things; I will put you in charge of many things. Share your master's joy!'…you should have deposited my money with the bankers… I would have received my money back with interest…"

The parable of the talents has so many lessons. God is the one that gives gifts, talents, even greatness of income. He trusts us to be trustworthy by doing something with what He gives us. The answer to the main question isn't why He decides what to give to whom but that we do something with it. What has God given you that you have buried. You sat on it long enough. It's time to make it happen. Don't you want to hear, "Well done"?

The rewards of recognizing that God could have given your gift and ability to anyone are plenteous. Imagine your talent on someone in your family. What would you say to them? What connections would you make for them so that they would achieve the greatness you know is in them? Would you remind them that God, the Creator of All, gave it to them for a reason? Would you encourage them that someone is waiting on their gift? You'd be right to do that and more. Now, do it for yourself!

It's important to note that the owner was upset with the one that buried his money. His remark that he should have at least gained interest is the topic for this week. Where are you storing your savings? Yes, you are holding it to reach a goal or for emergency purposes but make it work for you. There are too many banks that give you a minimal amount of return while using your money to loan to others and make great profit. Get the most from what you have amassed. Safe and secure is the savings and money market account. Do your research and move to a partnership that gives you the most. Check www.bankrate.com and compare. This week move to earn the maximum interest possible.

Divinely Connected: Steps to Fearless Financial Freedom

_____
1 Goal for the Week

Date: __/__/____
_____
Scripture/ Affirmation:

TOP 3 TASKS

- ○ _____
- ○ _____
- ○ _____

OTHER TO-DOS: **NOTES:**

Mindset _____

Goals _____

Budget _____

Spending _____

Eliminate _____

Automate _____

Debt _____

Credit _____

Giving _____

Savings _____

Investing _____

Business _____

Relationships _____

Family _____

Self Care _____

Luke 16:10-13 "Whoever is faithful in very little is also faithful in much..."

What do you chase after, God or money? As we look to prosper, we have to be careful that we are seeking for the right reasons. God is the one that makes prosperity possible and He is also the one that promises its availability to His children. There can be no greater joy to the heart of a father than to see his children doing well and walking in everything he has afforded for them. God's heart is for our abundant living!

A faithful Father is the one we serve. His desire is for our faithfulness too. From little to a lot we are tested so that we know our limits and the area we need to improve. Is your attitude different depending on what you have? Do you treat your brothers and sisters differently depending on what they can do for you? How do you handle working for and with someone else? Are you faithful to give your very best?

There is a story told of a contractor that did excellent work. He built mansions and entry level homes for so many but always paid close attention to detail. The owner of the company as the contractor was coming to retirement asked him to build one last house. The contractor did what was asked but he cut corners. He didn't put in the same level of precision that he had in all the other homes. When it was finally finished much to his surprise, the owner gave him that house. All along the owner had planned to bless him. Because the contractor didn't give his best, what he built for himself was not at the same level of excellence. Can you imagine him living in that house? Every time he looked in that corner with the counter unlevel he probably cringed. When he walked across the floor that had a dip that he didn't fill, he was reminded of how he wasn't faithful.

Don't let that be you! Do to the best of your ability everything that you put your hand to do. This includes overseeing the money God has blessed you to manage.

Divinely Connected: Steps to Fearless Financial Freedom

 # 1 Goal for the Week

Date: __/__/____

Scripture/ Affirmation:

TOP 3 TASKS

- _____
- _____
- _____

OTHER TO-DOS:

NOTES:

Mindset _____

Goals _____

Budget _____

Spending _____

Eliminate _____

Automate _____

Debt _____

Credit _____

Giving _____

Savings _____

Investing _____

Business _____

Relationships _____

Family _____

Self Care _____

Galatians 6:6-10 "… whatever a man sows he will also reap … So we must not get tired of doing good, for we will reap at the proper time if we don't give up. Therefore, as we have opportunity …"

God is good all the time, and all the time God is good! We know it, we quote it but do we emulate it? God is always doing good to us and through us. Count your blessings. Now reflect on the fact that while we were yet sinners He was doing good. When we didn't acknowledge Him, He still made ways in order that we would come to Him. As a good father, He has continued to hold fast to always giving us good. After all, every good gift comes from above.

It's gratitude journal time again! Yes, God has been good so document it. Leave it for others to see what He has done for you. When you look back over your life, you have to admit God has been good. No one else can tell it like you tell it. So, go tell it!

As you look at your overall financial plan, is there a place that you are doing good? Have you been consistent in doing good for others? Are you planning on leaving a legacy for your offspring? A good man/woman leaves an inheritance for his/her children's children.

This week review your plan and find ways of doing good. It may be setting an example for your children. It could be consistently saving so that your giving in the long run can increase. It could be adding a line item on your budget to include that charity you see on the front line. Whatever you find your hands to do, do it as unto the Lord.

Divinely Connected: Steps to Fearless Financial Freedom

1 Goal for the Week

Date: __/__/____

Scripture/ Affirmation:

TOP 3 TASKS

- ○ _____
- ○ _____
- ○ _____

OTHER TO-DOS:

NOTES:

Mindset _____

Goals _____

Budget _____

Spending _____

Eliminate _____

Automate _____

Debt _____

Credit _____

Giving _____

Savings _____

Investing _____

Business _____

Relationships _____

Family _____

Self Care _____

Divinely Connected: Steps to Fearless Financial Freedom

Psalm 24:1 "The earth and everything in it, the world and its inhabitants, belong to the Lord."

Looking heavenward for every good and perfect gift is the right posture. Everything belongs to God. He created all that we see. He also created you and me. When we have a need our first request should be to God. He owns the cattle on a thousand hills. There is nothing that is impossible for Him. God is our source!

Isn't it good to belong? Having a place to run for celebration and heartache is what we long for. Community. Connection. Commitment. God provides all of that and more. We have a refuge from the world. We have a strong tower that provides safety. We have light in the darkness and a balm in Gilead. Abiding in the secret place of the Most High allows for sanctuary that protects and provides. His grace is more than sufficient. His mercies being new every day. He is a father to the fatherless and a mother to the motherless. He takes us in and never leaves us or abandons us. He stands arms wide open ready to receive us. God is so good!

Who belongs to you? To whom do you belong? What makes up your family? Have you considered them in your financial plan? What provisions have you made to prepare them for the future? This week we are future focused. Review your goals, especially family goals. If you don't have a goal, then set a SMART goal. Make sure it is Specific, Measurable, Attainable, Relevant and Time based. You got this! Get the family involved and figure out their contribution too.

Everything belongs to God, so take care of what He has given you. Appreciate the gifts!

Divinely Connected: Steps to Fearless Financial Freedom

1 Goal for the Week

Date: __/__/____

Scripture/ Affirmation:

TOP 3 TASKS

- ○ _____
- ○ _____
- ○ _____

OTHER TO-DOS: **NOTES:**

Mindset _____

Goals _____

Budget _____

Spending _____

Eliminate _____

Automate _____

Debt _____

Credit _____

Giving _____

Savings _____

Investing _____

Business _____

Relationships _____

Family _____

Self Care _____

Divinely Connected: Steps to Fearless Financial Freedom

Matthew 22:21/ Mark 12:17/ Luke 20:25 "…Give back to Caesar the things that are Caesar's, and to God the things that are God's… "

What shall we render to God? What should we give to the One who has given all? Our hope is in God. Our trust, reliance and dependence is in God. We count on Him for every blessing. We lean on His faithfulness and stand on every single promise. We call His name late in the midnight hour. We cry unto Him in the middle of our desperation and we are confident that He hears us when we pray. Be grateful!

We praise God for all that He has done, will do and is doing. We acknowledge His presence and continue to need Him to be a way maker. We recognize His hand moving in our lives and expect that He is the miracle worker that never stops. For every mountain He brought you over, for every trial He's seen you through, for every blessing Hallelujah, for this we give Him praise! Be thankful!

Worship puts the focus and attention squarely where it belongs, on God! We ship to Him everything that He is worth. We declare that because of who He is we acknowledge Him. We recite His character traits and declare Him to be awesome in all of His ways. We call His name Jehovah! All that we need is in that name. He is the same yesterday, today and forever. We worship a great God and we should give Him all that He is due.

This week, commit to getting your giving to God right. All Kingdom work should be supported by those in the Kingdom. Help God's economy by being obedient to His word. Isn't He worthy?

Divinely Connected: Steps to Fearless Financial Freedom

1 Goal for the Week

Date: __/__/____

Scripture/ Affirmation:

TOP 3 TASKS

- ○ _____
- ○ _____
- ○ _____

OTHER TO-DOS:

NOTES:

Mindset _____

Goals _____

Budget _____

Spending _____

Eliminate _____

Automate _____

Debt _____

Credit _____

Giving _____

Savings _____

Investing _____

Business _____

Relationships _____

Family _____

Self Care _____

Divinely Connected: Steps to Fearless Financial Freedom

Mark 12:41-44 "… He watched… This poor widow has put in more than all those giving to the temple treasury. For they all gave out of their surplus, but she out of her poverty has put in everything she possessed – all she had to live on."

Giving is a big subject. What we give and what is given to us is all under scrutiny. The key here is that God watches what we give. Amazing to think that we can ball up a dollar to try to hide from others and God still sees it. Who are we fooling? God sees all, knows all and is over all!

Let's contemplate for a moment all that God has given to us. That gratitude journal came in handy to lift your spirits and refocus your attention. God has been so very good! When you consider all that He has done, then our sacrificing should be easy. Well, maybe acceptable or anticipated.

The eyes of the Lord are everywhere and He knows our heart. The thought of Him watching the offering… Well let's give our best! The amount of the gift wasn't as important as the attitude of the heart. Others can give more out of their abundance but when we give when it's a sacrifice now that gets God's attention.

This week praise God for all that He has done and then commit your heart to be a generous giver. It's time to evaluate both the tithe and the offering. Are you giving what your heart desires? Are you limiting your giving for selfish reasons? If you are actively re-evaluating your budget and things are tight, God knows. If you have been living in surplus and short changing God and His people, He knows that too. Get your heart right this week. Ask God for a clean heart and a right spirit toward His church and His people. Be your brother's keeper! Be a cheerful giver!

Divinely Connected: Steps to Fearless Financial Freedom

1 Goal for the Week

Date: __/__/____

Scripture/ Affirmation:

TOP 3 TASKS

- ○ _____
- ○ _____
- ○ _____

OTHER TO-DOS:

NOTES:

Mindset _____

Goals _____

Budget _____

Spending _____

Eliminate _____

Automate _____

Debt _____

Credit _____

Giving _____

Savings _____

Investing _____

Business _____

Relationships _____

Family _____

Self Care _____

Divinely Connected: Steps to Fearless Financial Freedom

Proverbs 3:9,10 "Honor the Lord with your possessions and with the first produce of your entire harvest; then your barns will be completely filled, and your vats will overflow with new wine."

Give honor to whom honor is due! We give prominence to those who have earned our esteem because we value them. We hold them in a place of high estimation because we recognize them as worthy. God is the one that deserves us to give Him glory and honor. He is worthy!

Is He worthy of all the praise? Is He worthy of the glory? Then show Him by honoring Him. As the verse says, we do it with our possessions and the first of what we have. Yes, God has given us everything that we have and we don't want to just give Him anything. We honor Him by giving our best! We put Him first. We esteem Him by our heart placing Him above our own needs and wants. We place a high value on God by showing Him tangibly with what He has given us stewardship over. We manage what God has given and we acknowledge Him by giving Him pre-eminence, first place. Decide today that from this point forward, God will have the first and the best. He is worthy!

We honor God in what we give to Kingdom causes and to others. As we honor God the one receiving the blessings also honors God because we acknowledge that we are His children. Blessings flow all around. It's an honor to be the one chosen to meet the need. It's a privilege to be seen as an angel working for God.

A story was told of a little homeless boy that prayed to God asking for help. A woman saw him looking in the window of a shoe store and he had no shoes. She invited him in and washed his feet, put socks on him, and bought him a pair of shoes. As they walked out of the store, he grabbed her hand and asked if she was God's wife. Oh, to be asked if you are related closely to God!

1 Goal for the Week

Date: __/__/____

Scripture/ Affirmation:

TOP 3 TASKS

- ○ _____
- ○ _____
- ○ _____

NOTES:

OTHER TO-DOS:

Mindset _____

Goals _____

Budget _____

Spending _____

Eliminate _____

Automate _____

Debt _____

Credit _____

Giving _____

Savings _____

Investing _____

Business _____

Relationships _____

Family _____

Self Care _____

John 10:10 "A thief comes only to steal and to kill and to destroy. I have come so that they may have life and have it in abundance."

Praise God for abundance! He promises to do exceeding, abundantly, above all that we could ask or think. That's abundance! Overflowing our expectations and going beyond even that is what God wants to do in and through us.

The God we serve loves us abundantly. He desires to hear us, protect us, provide for us and do for us what we can't do for ourselves. What a great shepherd! He gives and gives and gives. He protects His sheep. Others may come and go with their own selfish desires and ambition, but God is faithful. The one who sacrifices for us promises abundance on this side. Yes, eternal life awaits us but until we get there, He promises that His desire is for us to have a life in abundance. Live your best life!

Have you asked lately for the so much more that He wants to give you? Have you been seeking His presence? Have you knocked on the door of blessing? It's time. Stand on this promise that Jesus gave His life in order that we live an abundant life. Don't let it be in vain.

This week find the abundance. Look for the overflow and extra. Document the blessings of God and then decide if it is for you to keep or bless someone else. Remember, give and it shall be given to you pressed down, shaken together, and running over. Walk in your abundance and attract more!

Divinely Connected: Steps to Fearless Financial Freedom

1 Goal for the Week

Date: __/__/____

Scripture/ Affirmation:

TOP 3 TASKS

- _____
- _____
- _____

OTHER TO-DOS: **NOTES:**

Mindset _____

Goals _____

Budget _____

Spending _____

Eliminate _____

Automate _____

Debt _____

Credit _____

Giving _____

Savings _____

Investing _____

Business _____

Relationships _____

Family _____

Self Care _____

Divinely Connected: Steps to Fearless Financial Freedom

Exodus 16 - The Miracle of Manna

There is nothing like the miracles of the Old Testament: parting the Red Sea; the Jordan River; turning the bitter water sweet and the manna from heaven. We serve a miracle working God! Can you imagine walking on dry land where there was seconds before an ocean? Can you imagine your enemies being drowned in that same spot when the waters began to flow again? Ever thought of asking God for what is impossible and watching as He does the miraculous? Every day we see Him working even when we don't know He is working!

Complaints that we make about lack are really directed to the One who supplies all of our needs. Often we criticize the Israelites because God worked one miracle after another for them and then 3 days later they were complaining again. Are you a chronic complainer? Are your grateful thoughts only momentary? We are to do all things without murmuring and complaining but that seems a tall order. We can ask without complaining but the attitude of 'if you were so good you would' becomes a complaint.

Looking back at what was or even looking around at what someone else has is the wrong direction. Our focus should be vertical asking God for all of our needs. He is the giver of every good gift. He is our source. He alone is our ultimate provider. Focus on God's direction and follow closely His commands for the blessings to flow. Manna from heaven? The heavenly intervention to feed the soul. Just enough until... Are you ready to get to the borders of until? Day by day God provided for 40 years. Every need was met until. Wait on God and you will get to the border of Canaan, a land flowing with milk and honey. From just enough to overflowing is your destiny!

Divinely Connected: Steps to Fearless Financial Freedom

1 Goal for the Week

Date: __/__/____

Scripture/ Affirmation:

TOP 3 TASKS

- _____
- _____
- _____

OTHER TO-DOS:

NOTES:

Mindset _____

Goals _____

Budget _____

Spending _____

Eliminate _____

Automate _____

Debt _____

Credit _____

Giving _____

Savings _____

Investing _____

Business _____

Relationships _____

Family _____

Self Care _____

Divinely Connected: Steps to Fearless Financial Freedom

Matthew 6:25-33 "… Isn't life more than food and the body more than clothing?... your heavenly Father knows that you need them. But seek first the kingdom of God and His righteousness, and all these things will be provided for you."

Dependency on God for all is the meditation for today. Yes, you have needs! God knows and He promises to provide. The prerequisite is to seek Him first and His righteousness.

Seeking God's presence in every situation may not seem easy initially. How often do we go into a meeting with our own agenda? How many times have you gone to work without praying? How many frustrated phone calls have you had and then realized you didn't ask God to intervene? Actively seeking God and His wisdom before any event and in everything allows us to be at peace. There is peace in His presence.

We are told to be anxious for nothing but in everything by prayer and petition to make our requests known to God and He promises to give us His peace. He tells us to come unto Him all that labor and are heavy laden and He will give us rest (peace). We are to walk with our feet wrapped with the preparation of the gospel of peace. Peace is to be obtained in every situation and circumstance. We get God's peace when our dependence and trust is in Him. Will He come through? You bet! Will He be early? Probably not. Will you have to wait? Sometimes. But even when you don't see Him working, He is still working! Even when you don't feel Him working, He is still working! He's the God of more than enough. He is able! He's our miracle worker, promise keeper, light in the darkness. That's the God we serve!

Now seek Him (for wisdom) and right standing with Him (for your heart issues). His character should be imitated! Others should see glimpses of God in you. You should be a reflection of His glory. Your stewardship, ability to manage what He has entrusted to you, should be a representation of the God that you serve. This week see if you can see God in what you are doing.

Divinely Connected: Steps to Fearless Financial Freedom

1 Goal for the Week

Date: __/__/____

Scripture/ Affirmation:

TOP 3 TASKS

- _____
- _____
- _____

OTHER TO-DOS: **NOTES:**

Mindset _____

Goals _____

Budget _____

Spending _____

Eliminate _____

Automate _____

Debt _____

Credit _____

Giving _____

Savings _____

Investing _____

Business _____

Relationships _____

Family _____

Self Care _____

Divinely Connected: Steps to Fearless Financial Freedom

Matthew 6:11 "Give us today our daily bread"

Every day there is a need to look to God for provision for the day. Nothing more than just 24 hours sometimes is all we can ask. Isn't it great that we serve a God that is more than able to provide! One who knows what you have need of and provides for you better than you could have asked if you had the words. Amazingly God always comes through!

As the children of Israel wandered in the wilderness, God provided manna from heaven for them daily. They were to take what was enough for the day. It reminded them of their daily dependence. Sometimes we can get so caught up in our own thinking and planning that we forget to consult the one that gives the greatest counsel. A simple, 'Help Lord', is a prayer that can make the difference and change the atmosphere. How often do we forget we need daily instructions? We can get so busy that we overlook our greatest asset. We value things and people and are remiss in acknowledging the One that gave us the things and the people. God is our source and everything else is a resource. Put Him first!

Bread is symbolic of our necessity for nourishment. The food that sustains the body giving us energy and the ability to live. It is a vital requirement for life itself. God is the essential element that we need on a regular basis. He knows the plans He has for you. He knows what you are going through. He knows.

He gives hope for tomorrow, joy for your sorrow and strength for everything you go through. He knows the plans He has for you!

This week ask for daily bread. Ask and it shall be given to you.

It's budget review time again. How much are you spending daily on the necessities. Make changes as necessary. Don't forget the eating out and the buying of lunch. Thank God that all your needs are met!

Divinely Connected: Steps to Fearless Financial Freedom

1 Goal for the Week

Date: __/__/____

Scripture/ Affirmation:

TOP 3 TASKS

- ○ _____
- ○ _____
- ○ _____

OTHER TO-DOS:

NOTES:

Mindset _____

Goals _____

Budget _____

Spending _____

Eliminate _____

Automate _____

Debt _____

Credit _____

Giving _____

Savings _____

Investing _____

Business _____

Relationships _____

Family _____

Self Care _____

Acts 3:6 "But Peter said, 'I don't have silver or gold, but what I have, I give you: In the names of Jesus Christ the Nazarene, get up and walk!'"

Aren't you grateful that God doesn't give us what we expect but exceeds our expectations? We get caught up sometimes in what we have always done that was satisfactory. The God we serve reminds us that satisfactory is not His desire for us. He has excellence in mind for you!

Can you imagine God dreaming about where He wants to take you? Do you ever wonder why He chose you? What He has in store for you is absolutely amazing!

Have you ever felt the push from God to move along? You know He sometimes whispers that there is more. Sometimes if you are stubborn enough and the horse is dead, He pushes you off because you wouldn't dismount. He reminds us in His word that His thoughts are not our thoughts and His plans for us are for our good. He has a great plan that we haven't even fathomed. You've read that eye hasn't seen and ear hasn't heard neither has it entered into the heart of man what God has planned for us. Your family, your friends, even your enemies don't have a clue how valuable and anointed you are! That's the plan God has. Now get on board!

To get up from your current state will require you to set goals that only God can come through on. This week dream big. Bigger than you've ever imagined. Make it a goal that is beyond you and will impact and influence so many others. Write down goals for family and legacy as well as general goals. Don't forget the savings and investing piece. Keep in mind your giving as well. You got this! You are walking victoriously and in abundance!

Divinely Connected: Steps to Fearless Financial Freedom

1 Goal for the Week

Date: __/__/____

Scripture/ Affirmation:

TOP 3 TASKS

- ○ _____
- ○ _____
- ○ _____

OTHER TO-DOS:

NOTES:

Mindset _____

Goals _____

Budget _____

Spending _____

Eliminate _____

Automate _____

Debt _____

Credit _____

Giving _____

Savings _____

Investing _____

Business _____

Relationships _____

Family _____

Self Care _____

Divinely Connected: Steps to Fearless Financial Freedom

Isaiah 55:8-11 "'My thoughts are not your thoughts, and your ways are not My ways'... My ways are higher... saturating the earth and making it germinate and sprout, and providing seed to sow and food to eat, so My word that comes from My mouth will not return to Me empty, but it will accomplish what I please and will prosper in what I send it to do."

Blessing upon blessings! That's what the Lord pours out upon us. His word that He has spoken over your life shall come to pass. It will not return to Him void and without effect. God promises and His promises are His words that He has spoken. They will fill the earth and saturate every part of your life. Not only will your life be watered but it will produce according as He has spoken. It will be nourishment for you and impact those you sow into. May His favor be upon you!

Consider what God has said about you. He formed you in your mother's womb. He knew you before the foundation of the world. He hand picked you and adopted you into the family. He has blessed you with all spiritual blessings. His favor is upon you for a thousand generations. If God be for you, who can be against you! As He has said eye hasn't seen it yet. His plans for you are for good and not evil. He plans to give you hope and a future. You are never alone because He promised to never leave you nor abandon you. You are the apple of His eye. He constantly watches over you. He holds you in the palm of His hand protecting and comforting you. He even sends His angels to have charge over you to keep you in all your ways. God loves you with an everlasting love! He even sent Jesus to die for you so that He could have a relationship with you. You are so valuable to God and to the Kingdom. Now think on these things!

This week bask in the presence of God and all that He has spoken. It shall come to pass!

Divinely Connected: Steps to Fearless Financial Freedom

1 Goal for the Week

Date: __/__/____

Scripture/ Affirmation:

TOP 3 TASKS

- _____
- _____
- _____

OTHER TO-DOS:

NOTES:

Mindset _____

Goals _____

Budget _____

Spending _____

Eliminate _____

Automate _____

Debt _____

Credit _____

Giving _____

Savings _____

Investing _____

Business _____

Relationships _____

Family _____

Self Care _____

Divinely Connected: Steps to Fearless Financial Freedom

Mark 4:26-29 "'The kingdom of God is like this,' He said, 'A man scatters seed on the ground; he sleeps and rises – night and day, any the seed sprouts and grows – he doesn't know how. The soil produces a crop by itself – first the blade, then the head, and then the ripe grain on the head. But as soon as the crop is ready, he sends for the sickle, because the harvest has come.'"

Expect great things! Have you ever considered that we have no idea how much of life works? You plant a seed, it grows and then you reap a harvest. Do you know where the seed originated? When you planted it, did you know how it grew? We can watch it but we don't know exactly how to re-create without the intervention of God. All we know is that at the end of the season, a crop is produced and harvested.

Such is the way God works in our lives. We pray, planting seeds expecting great things. We don't know how or when God will work it out, yet great things. When we don't see Him working, He is still working. When we don't feel Him working, He's still working. When He heals unexpectedly, He's working. When that child comes home after going down a path of destruction, great things. Late in the midnight hour as He turns it around, we see His handiwork. Every time you turn around He is blessing. A simple smile, an unexpected check, a gift just because or a marriage restored, all are blessings from God. You planted the seed and the harvest has come. Praise God for the harvest! He is the Lord of the harvest!

This week review your harvest. Praise God for what He has multiplied in your life and your finances. It's praise break week. Give Him what He is due!

Divinely Connected: Steps to Fearless Financial Freedom

1 Goal for the Week

Date: __/__/____

Scripture/ Affirmation:

TOP 3 TASKS

- ○ _____
- ○ _____
- ○ _____

OTHER TO-DOS:

NOTES:

Mindset _____

Goals _____

Budget _____

Spending _____

Eliminate _____

Automate _____

Debt _____

Credit _____

Giving _____

Savings _____

Investing _____

Business _____

Relationships _____

Family _____

Self Care _____

Divinely Connected: Steps to Fearless Financial Freedom

Hebrews 11:6 "Now without faith it is impossible to please God, for the one who draws near to Him must believe that He exists and rewards those who seek Him."

Faith in God says that we trust, rely and depend upon Him. How dependent are you? Is your hope in Him? Have you removed the plan B and made the one and only plan the one that agrees with God's will?

Trusting God shows that the heavy lifting belongs to Him. Relying on the word and works of God sounds easy but in practice not so much. In order to build your faith, look at all God has done.

Amazing grace how sweet the sound that saved a wretch like me. He is able to save to the uttermost. It doesn't matter what you've done in the past, God promises forgiveness to those who repent. He cleanses us of all unrighteousness as we confess our sins. He promises wisdom to those who ask. He is our counselor that knows the end before the beginning. He is a protector that provides refuge and a strong tower for us to run to in the time of trouble. He promises to hide us in a secret place. He provides light in the darkness and a way where there doesn't seem to be a way. He keeps all His promises and there are a multitude of them in the Bible. He brings joy in the midst of sorrow. He promises beauty for ashes and turns our mourning into dancing. Though trouble comes, He promises that it won't last always. Weeping He says may endure for a night but joy will come in the morning. He even sends a rainbow to remind us that He won't flood the earth again. God has sent many signs of His faithfulness and His love toward us. Trust His word and His ability. He is! And He rewards!

This week ask specifically for God to intervene in your finances. Whether it's more income, better planning or debt reduction turn it over to God.

Divinely Connected: Steps to Fearless Financial Freedom

1 Goal for the Week

Date: __/__/____

Scripture/ Affirmation:

TOP 3 TASKS

- ○ _____
- ○ _____
- ○ _____

OTHER TO-DOS:

NOTES:

Mindset _____

Goals _____

Budget _____

Spending _____

Eliminate _____

Automate _____

Debt _____

Credit _____

Giving _____

Savings _____

Investing _____

Business _____

Relationships _____

Family _____

Self Care _____

John 6:6-13 "…'There's a boy here who has five barley loaves and two fish – but what are they for so many?'… Jesus took the loaves, and after giving thanks He distributed them to those who were seated – so also with the fish, as much as they wanted … 'Collect the leftovers so that nothing is wasted'…"

Whatever you put in the Master's hand will be multiplied! Have you ever thought you didn't have enough and then miraculously it was more than enough? Has God ever intervened like the story of the *Happy Meal* feeding 5000 men plus women and children?

The God we serve is not only faithful to meet our needs but He often exceeds them. Such a little amount amongst so many is what appears in the natural. Giving the chance for God to add His super to the natural produces miracles. Can He do it again? You bet! His promise still stands, great is His faithfulness. Every need shall be supplied. He has never failed you yet.

This week collect the leftovers. All the areas that seem minor are pockets to reap a harvest. Check your utilities, look for ways to save. Energy audits, not running the shower as long; look for ways you have unintentionally caused your bills to be higher. Then check all recurring charges. Are you still using that membership? Can the cable bill, car insurance and others be reduced? Are you watching all those channels? Re-evaluate your monthly automatic spending. Collect the leftovers. Contact your providers to see if the rates have improved.

If you have a home mortgage consider paying every 2 weeks (bi-monthly). If your mortgage lender doesn't offer it, you can set it up yourself. On the 15th of the month pay half of your regular payment ahead of time. Then on the 1st of the month pay the other half. You just saved yourself some interest! Continue doing this and watch your balance dwindle quickly.

Thank God for the leftovers!

Divinely Connected: Steps to Fearless Financial Freedom

 # 1 Goal for the Week

Date: __/__/____

Scripture/ Affirmation:

TOP 3 TASKS

- ○ _____
- ○ _____
- ○ _____

OTHER TO-DOS: **NOTES:**

Mindset _____

Goals   _____

Budget _____

Spending _____

Eliminate _____

Automate _____

Debt _____

Credit   _____

Giving   _____

Savings _____

Investing _____

Business _____

Relationships _____

Family   _____

Self Care _____

Matthew 12:29 "How can someone enter a strong man's house and steal his possessions unless he first ties up the strong man? Then he can rob his house."

God promises us that His kingdom is not of this world. He admonishes us not to be conformed to this world but to be transformed by the renewing of our minds. We need a mindset shift!

We are given authority to cast down imaginations and to bring into captivity all thoughts under the obedience of Christ (2 Corinthians 10:5). We need a Kingdom mindset. Be committed this week to follow God's word. Stay in covenant relationship. No co-signing. Trust in God for all your provision and believe that He will supply all your needs according to His riches.

There are many systems of the world that are set against you in order to constantly deplete your finances. You've taken the time to review the areas to gain back the leftovers but there are systems designed for your destruction. Consider all the credit card applications that come in the mail. If you are in debt now, don't open another card. The interest rate alone is causing you to pay more for the item than it is worth. If you are not carrying a balance on your card and are paying it off every month, great! If you do have a balance, do everything you can to pay more than the minimum and don't get another card. If you have multiple cards, attempt to consolidate the total amount due on one card. As an example: if you have 3 cards each with a minimum of $50 due, that's $150 just in the minimum payment. If your total balance was on one card you may only have a minimum of $90. The extra $60 would be going to pay down the balance.

This week clear the credit card debt. Consolidate to use only one card if possible. If you are maxed out, try opening a new one with your bank at a lower interest rate but enough to cover all the balances if they allow the transfer.

Divinely Connected: Steps to Fearless Financial Freedom

1 Goal for the Week

Date: __/__/____

Scripture/ Affirmation:

TOP 3 TASKS

- _____
- _____
- _____

OTHER TO-DOS: **NOTES:**

Mindset _____

Goals _____

Budget _____

Spending _____

Eliminate _____

Automate _____

Debt _____

Credit _____

Giving _____

Savings _____

Investing _____

Business _____

Relationships _____

Family _____

Self Care _____

Divinely Connected: Steps to Fearless Financial Freedom

Haggai 1:5-9 "... 'Think carefully about your ways: You have planted much but harvested little. You eat but never have enough to be satisfied. You drink but never have enough to become drunk. You put on clothes but never have enough to get warm. The wage earner puts his wages into a bag with a hole in it.' ... 'You expected much, but then it amounted to little ... Because My house still lies in ruins, while each of you is busy with his own house... '"

What is the priority? Why do we work so hard to only have little to show for it? Could it be that we have our priorities out of order? Is it possible that God is withholding our blessing or actually we are having our blessings held up because of our own actions?

God's desire is that we prosper and be in good health. He has favored many over the years that whatever their hands touched turned to gold. Things prosper under the direction of those who are committed to God. The good news is that this too can be you! God promises that as we come to Him, He will answer and give us wisdom. Could it be that you are the cause of your own struggle? Then it's time to get it right!

This week evaluate your giving to the Kingdom. A good steward is one that manages well what was entrusted to him/her by the Master. We give time, talent and treasures. Are you giving God your time consisting of your own devotion and prayer? Are you using the gifts He has bestowed upon you for the Kingdom? Now what about the giving? God gave all to us and asks that we acknowledge Him and put Him first. This is seen in the tithe and offering. Tithe being 10% of your income should be given to the church where you are fed spiritually. Any other giving is identified as offering and should be given to the church(es) and other charitable organizations that support a Kingdom agenda. Align your giving so that you focus on Kingdom. Watch God remove some of the struggle!

Divinely Connected: Steps to Fearless Financial Freedom

1 Goal for the Week

Date: __/__/____

Scripture/ Affirmation:

TOP 3 TASKS

- ○ _____
- ○ _____
- ○ _____

OTHER TO-DOS:

NOTES:

Mindset _____

Goals _____

Budget _____

Spending _____

Eliminate _____

Automate _____

Debt _____

Credit _____

Giving _____

Savings _____

Investing _____

Business _____

Relationships _____

Family _____

Self Care _____

Malachi 3:10-11 "'... Bring the full tenth into the storehouse so that there may be food in My house. Test Me in this way' says the Lord of Hosts. 'See if I will not open the floodgates of heaven and pour out a blessing for you without measure. I will rebuke the devourer for you, so that it will not ruin the produce of your land and your vine in your field will not fail to produce fruit,' says the Lord of Hosts."

Promises, promises! The Lord promises us that if we are obedient in covenant relationship that there will be an abundance of blessings poured out on us. Not only will there be a plethora of provision but the hand of the enemy will be held at bay as to not ruin what we have. That's great news!

Often we want the promises without meeting the prerequisites. In God's economy the tithe or ten percent is given to take care of those who are serving in the Kingdom. Those who minister and take account for the spiritual food that is needed to encourage the body of Christ partake of the gifts given. In addition, those who are strangers, orphans, and others in need are taken care of from the offerings given. If the tithe and offerings are withheld then how can one expect the servants to be able to serve? How can one expect to come to the house of God and find refreshment when times are tough? How can we shine light in a dark world without being able to meet the physical need first? The giving and acknowledging God first is a heart matter that sets the believer up to make a great impact. Not only will the giver be blessed for giving but the receiver will also glorify God because of the gift. Blessings all around!

This week look at your tithe again and make sure it is based on your gross income (before deductions). This way you can make sure you are giving God what is due Him. You set yourself up to not only prove that God will come through but to receive a multitude of blessings with protection.

Divinely Connected: Steps to Fearless Financial Freedom

1 Goal for the Week

Date: __/__/____

Scripture/ Affirmation:

TOP 3 TASKS

- _____
- _____
- _____

OTHER TO-DOS: **NOTES:**

Mindset   _____

Goals   _____

Budget   _____

Spending   _____

Eliminate   _____

Automate   _____

Debt   _____

Credit   _____

Giving   _____

Savings   _____

Investing   _____

Business   _____

Relationships _____

Family   _____

Self Care   _____

Divinely Connected: Steps to Fearless Financial Freedom

Psalm 91:11 "For He will give His angels orders concerning you, to protect you in all your ways."

Angelic protection is a promise from God! Have you considered that He has given the angels orders to watch over all that concerns you? Imagine them stationed around you and your family.

Our Father is such a protector that not only is He looking out for us but He has the heavenly host at His disposal to make sure they also stand guard. Can you say we are never alone! That is comforting news. God protects what belongs to Him and that includes us. We are under witness protection!

Pray for your eyes to be opened to see! In 2 Kings the 6th chapter, Elisha prayed that the eyes of the young man be opened to see all that were with them. Sometimes it appears that we are alone and trouble is on every side. God has a host of help for us. He promises that when we are in trouble, He will raise up a standard against our enemies. He said we can find grace and help in a time of need. We are given the opportunity to come boldly before His throne and ask for help. No pretense just bringing all of our concerns. We can cast the whole of our care upon Him because He cares for us. Pray that God open the eyes of your heart so that you can see Him as He is… a Good Good Father!

This week ask God to show you what you do not see. Family, Finances and your Future are up for revelation this week. Allow Him to speak to you in dreams and visions … then write it down. Goals may be given… opportunities on the horizon … even areas to cut from your budget. Let God speak and then you follow through by walking it out!

Divinely Connected: Steps to Fearless Financial Freedom

1 Goal for the Week

Date: __/__/____

Scripture/ Affirmation:

TOP 3 TASKS

- _____
- _____
- _____

OTHER TO-DOS:

NOTES:

Mindset _____

Goals _____

Budget _____

Spending _____

Eliminate _____

Automate _____

Debt _____

Credit _____

Giving _____

Savings _____

Investing _____

Business _____

Relationships _____

Family _____

Self Care _____

Divinely Connected: Steps to Fearless Financial Freedom

Matthew 7:24-25 "Therefore, everyone who hears these words of Mine and acts on them will be like a sensible man who built his house on the rock. The rain fell, the rivers rose, and the winds blew and pounded that house. Yet it didn't collapse, because its foundation was on the rock."

As we put feet to our faith we stand on the foundation of God's word. We walk based on His promises. Blessed be the name of the Lord!

Trials may come and at some point it may seem like hurricane proportions arise in our lives. The good news is that if our foundation is sure, we don't worry. God promises that everything will work out for our good to those that love Him and the ones called according to His purpose.

Cakes are so good! Regardless of which cake you like best, each ingredient in the cake mix doesn't necessarily taste good. Who wants to eat a handful of flour? What about raw eggs? The sugar may be sweet but we know helpings of it isn't good for us. Every ingredient has its place. The baking soda, the vanilla extract all play a part in making sure the final outcome is delicious. Cake batter may be tempting as you lick the spoon but ultimately the best is still yet to come. As the batter bakes in the oven you get a whiff of joy. The oven is hot but it also serves a purpose. The finished product is representative of working it all out for our good. We may not like the individual situations that come in our life but we have to admit that it allowed us to grow spiritually. You wouldn't be as strong in the faith without the circumstances you have overcome.

Consider this week all that you have overcome. God is our rock and our foundation. You fall not, because He is always there to support you!

This week evaluate your financial foundation. Do you have enough cash as a base? Is your emergency fund fully funded? Are you saving regularly? Have you put aside 6-9 months of gross income? That's your goal... make a plan!

Divinely Connected: Steps to Fearless Financial Freedom

1 Goal for the Week

Date: __/__/____

Scripture/ Affirmation:

TOP 3 TASKS

- ○ _____
- ○ _____
- ○ _____

OTHER TO-DOS: NOTES:

Mindset _____

Goals _____

Budget _____

Spending _____

Eliminate _____

Automate _____

Debt _____

Credit _____

Giving _____

Savings _____

Investing _____

Business _____

Relationships _____

Family _____

Self Care _____

1 Kings 17 – "… I have commanded the ravens to provide for you there… The ravens kept bringing him bread and meat in the morning and in the evening, and he drank from the wadi… Look, I have commanded a woman who is a widow to provide for you there… I don't have anything baked – only a handful of flour in the jar and a bit of oil in the jug… The flour jar will not become empty and the jug will not run dry… the woman, Elijah, and her household ate for many days… "

Miracle provisions! Looking back over the past we know God is a God of miracles. He provides for those that are His. Whether it is miracle bread from heaven, a Happy Meal that feeds thousands, or a dirty bird that brings breakfast and dinner, our God is able to meet all of our needs. He promised that He would supply! He asks that we seek His kingdom and His righteousness and all things will be added. Can you imagine your oil never running out? What about the ability to see your provision continuing many days? Can He do it again? Absolutely. If you are in need of a miracle, just look to the only One who's able.

Are miracles happening today? Yes! Each morning we wake up is an indication that the finger of God touched us. We get new mercies every day. His grace follows us and His favor in small and great things are ever present. What miracles have occurred in your life? What miracles are you anticipating? Now is the time to thank God that He is able and ask for the impossible.

This week look for the miracles and ask for new ones. Ask God to show Himself strong in your life in such a way that you can be a testimony for others to read. When it comes to your finances, ask Him to turn them around for the better. Ask for miracles in debt elimination. Ask for increase. This is your week.

Divinely Connected: Steps to Fearless Financial Freedom

 # 1 Goal for the Week

Date: __/__/____

Scripture/ Affirmation:

TOP 3 TASKS

- ○ _____
- ○ _____
- ○ _____

OTHER TO-DOS:

NOTES:

Mindset _____

Goals _____

Budget _____

Spending _____

Eliminate _____

Automate _____

Debt _____

Credit _____

Giving _____

Savings _____

Investing _____

Business _____

Relationships _____

Family _____

Self Care _____

Divinely Connected: Steps to Fearless Financial Freedom

Obadiah 17-21 "But there will be a deliverance on Mount Zion, and it will be holy; the house of Jacob will dispossess those who dispossessed them… the kingdom will be the Lord's."

The Lord is just! What the enemy has taken will be returned. As we get our minds right and follow what God has prescribed, we stand to recover all. There is a great reversal on the horizon. We, as the children of God, will possess what the Lord has promised. It's time to walk in victory! Whatever God has for you is for you!

The past may show signs of the enemy taking territory because of ignorance, lack of discipline or simply bad decisions. No matter what the reason, as we look into the Word and follow what it says there are promises that God stands behind. He promises that He is just. He makes wrong things right. He corrects crooked paths and makes them straight. He is able to do what seems impossible to man. The earth is the Lord's and His kingdom will stand and endure forever.

This week concentrate on the God that is a righteous judge. The One that sits high and looks low. He holds you in the palm of His hands and stands ready to assist. He is the sure foundation. He is the King of Kings and the Lord of Lords. The One that owns the earth and all things in it. The One that loves you to wholeness and stands ready to erase the mistakes of the past. He offers forgiveness. Receive it now.

This week look at any past bad decisions. Not for condemnation but to not repeat the same mistakes. This week you are to eliminate what is hindering you. Mindset. Debt. Weights that belong to others. Feel the freedom!

Divinely Connected: Steps to Fearless Financial Freedom

1 Goal for the Week

Date: __/__/____

Scripture/ Affirmation:

TOP 3 TASKS

- ○ _____
- ○ _____
- ○ _____

OTHER TO-DOS:

NOTES:

Mindset _____

Goals _____

Budget _____

Spending _____

Eliminate _____

Automate _____

Debt _____

Credit _____

Giving _____

Savings _____

Investing _____

Business _____

Relationships _____

Family _____

Self Care _____

Numbers 20:7-12 "... You will bring water for them from the rock and provide drink for the community and their livestock..."

Exodus 15:23 -27 "They came to Marah, but hey could not drink the water at Marah because it was bitter... the water became drinkable... 'If you will carefully obey the Lord your God, do what is right in His eyes, pay attention to His commands, and keep all His statutes... I am Yahweh who heals you'"

God is the one that can bring provision from unexpected places! Can you imagine water coming from a rock in abundance that it takes care of you and all that concerns you? Unexpected provision is on the way this week. That's the God that we serve. When we put Him at the center of it all, He comes in and miracles happen.

Our God is also able to turn any current bitter situation sweet. He is able to work all things out for our good and His glory. It doesn't matter what it looks like now, there is victory ahead. When everything revolves around the God we serve, nothing else matters. Because God is able to turn things around and cover us, we call on the One that can make the changes necessary.

Won't it be sweet to put the past behind you. Won't it be grand to be financially free. * Debt eliminated * Saving automated. *Bills paid before they are due. * Money completely managed.

This week it's time to get everything in order. Your financial plan needs teeth so it's not just a wish. Determine what you need to do and plan to put feet to your faith. Believe God will make a way and then ask Him to give you direction.

Divinely Connected: Steps to Fearless Financial Freedom

1 Goal for the Week

Date: __/__/____

Scripture/ Affirmation:

TOP 3 TASKS

- ○ _____
- ○ _____
- ○ _____

OTHER TO-DOS:

NOTES:

Mindset _____

Goals _____

Budget _____

Spending _____

Eliminate _____

Automate _____

Debt _____

Credit _____

Giving _____

Savings _____

Investing _____

Business _____

Relationships _____

Family _____

Self Care _____

Genesis 15:1 "…I am your shield; your reward will be very great"

Amaze us God! Take our breath away! The promises that God makes are fantastic. He promises that He is our shield. He stands guard over everything and always watches out for us. God is amazing in that He stands in between us and what is coming against us. That's great news! Not only am I not alone but I have a divine protector who's determined to protect me at all cost. My Lord, my shield!

We not only have protection but we also have provision. God reminds us that we were young and now we are old and we have never seen the righteous forsaken nor his seed begging bread. What a promise! It may appear momentarily that the land of just enough is your dwelling place but following God's principles leads to a land of abundance. He says His reward for us is very great. He is our exceeding great reward. Whatever we have done, sacrificed for and invested in, God promises that there will be a return on our investment. This return is going to be very great. No matter how long it takes, wait on it. It shall come to pass. Expect greater!

In the middle of a world crisis it may seem that the waters have stopped flowing and the dam is holding back the floods, but the floods are going to be released. There will come a day, in due time, when everything you have planted and watered will bring forth an increase. Everything we ask according to God's will shall come to pass in His season. Though it tarry, wait on it. God has not failed yet and He never will. He is able and can be trusted.

This week trust God to establish in your finances a hedge of protection. Look for ways to secure your income. This may mean removing recurring charges. It could be that some decisions need to re-evaluated. Renegotiate large contracts/mortgages. Make provision to allow God to be your shield. Be ready to receive the very great reward!

Divinely Connected: Steps to Fearless Financial Freedom

1 Goal for the Week

Date: __/__/____

Scripture/ Affirmation:

TOP 3 TASKS

- ○ _____
- ○ _____
- ○ _____

OTHER TO-DOS: **NOTES:**

Mindset   _____

Goals   _____

Budget _____

Spending   _____

Eliminate _____

Automate   _____

Debt   _____

Credit   _____

Giving   _____

Savings   _____

Investing _____

Business _____

Relationships _____

Family   _____

Self Care   _____

Habakkuk 2:2-3 "The Lord answered me: Write down this vision; clearly inscribe it on tablets so one may easily read it. For the vision is yet for the appointed time; it testifies about the end and will not lie. Though it delays, wait for it, since it will certainly come and not be late."

Thank you God for vision! Clear vision! Has God spoken to you about your life, your family and your finances? Has He ordered your steps in your business? Has He directed you regarding your gifts? God speaks and we should listen.

The visions God gives are not minor easily attainable imaginations. Usually they seem enormous, greater than anything one can accomplish on their own. Often it involves areas that you don't have all knowledge and will need assistance to do. Ultimately it is going to require divine intervention. That's how you know it is a God given vision, it can't be accomplished by one human in a short time. So, what is the vision? Write it down!

The God we serve when He gives a vision will also give the provision for what He orders. Thank Him for His grace and faithfulness! God's grace covers the areas we are unsure of and He gives favor in the areas that we need. Imagine the God of the entire universe that created all that we see, oceans, sky, clouds, and rainbows still thought He needed one of you! You are a valuable piece in the equation. Go ahead and step into it! He built you for this!

This week write down the vision. Set your God sized goals and watch God intervene to achieve them. If you don't know what to write, take a moment to ask God to speak to you. If you start with something smaller, that's ok just begin. Write the vision as clearly as you can. Keep writing! Keep asking! Document it all. This is our starting point and it will be a testimony when all is said and done. Get ready to watch God show out on your behalf!

Divinely Connected: Steps to Fearless Financial Freedom

1 Goal for the Week

Date: __/__/____

Scripture/ Affirmation:

TOP 3 TASKS

- _____
- _____
- _____

OTHER TO-DOS:

NOTES:

Mindset _____

Goals _____

Budget _____

Spending _____

Eliminate _____

Automate _____

Debt _____

Credit _____

Giving _____

Savings _____

Investing _____

Business _____

Relationships _____

Family _____

Self Care _____

Divinely Connected: Steps to Fearless Financial Freedom

Looking for your next step to gain total financial success?
https://h2htruth.org/counseling-1

Also available:

Family Worship:
Reaching All Who Attend   ISBN 9781436370158

Financial Wisdom For Financial Freedom
    ISBN 9780999173305
    ISBN 9780999173312

Not Just Paper   ISBN 9780999173329
    ISBN 9780999173336

www.H2HTruth.org

Podcast – heart2hearttruth

www.linkedin.com/in/chonta-haynes
www.instagram.com/ctahaynes
www.pinterest.com/chontah/messages
www.facebook.com/chonta.haynes
www.facebook.com/h2htruth
www.twitter.com/chonta_haynes

Heart 2 Heart Truth Foundation 501 (c) 3

God has provided opportunities to meet the needs of others and bring the Gospel in a practical way. Dr. Haynes' books have been distributed through the library system, churches and Christian colleges to serve the larger population.

Additional *Divinely Connected* devotionals coming soon

www.ingramcontent.com/pod-product-compliance
Lightning Source LLC
Chambersburg PA
CBHW050437010526
44118CB00013B/1575